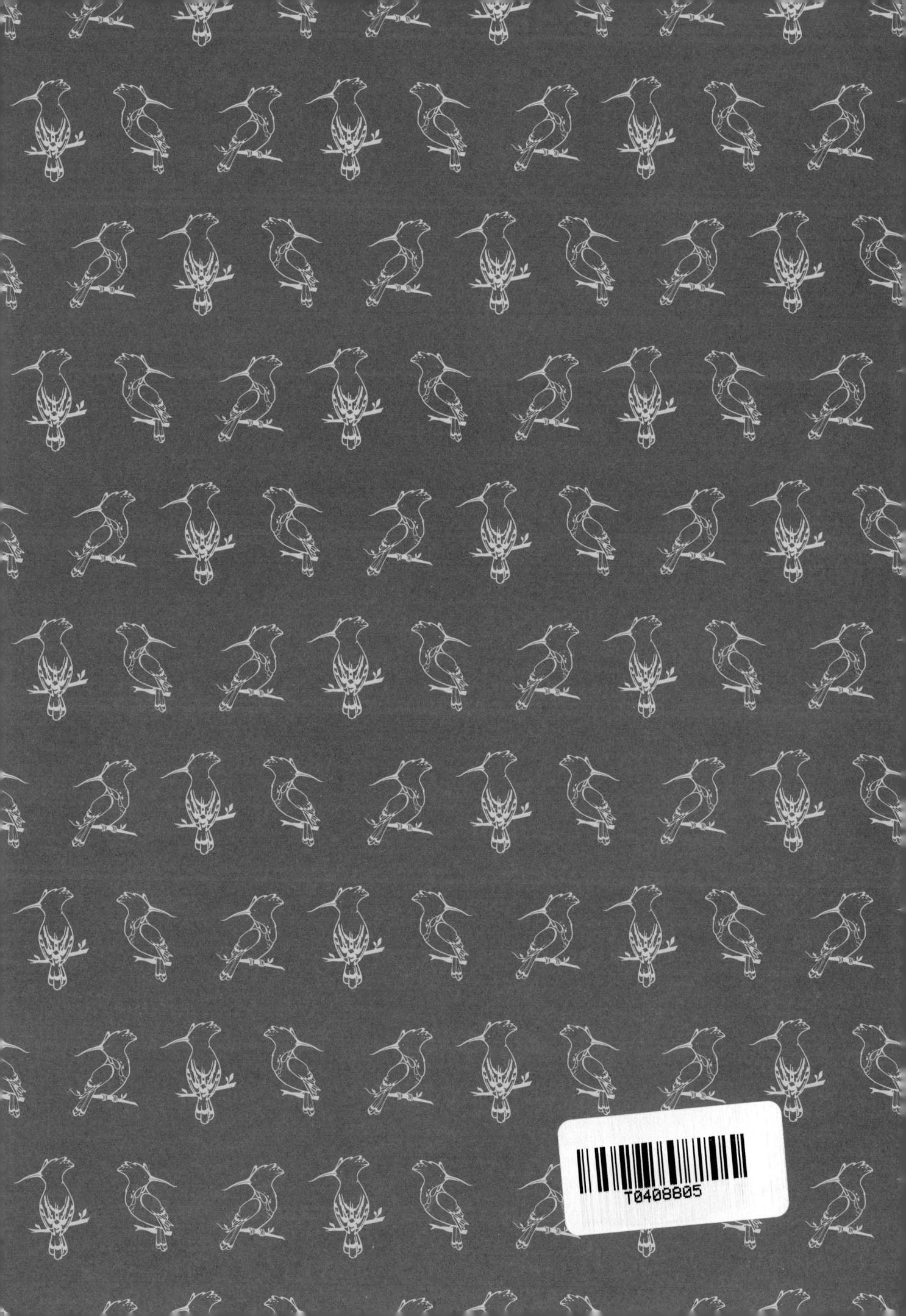

First published in the United Kingdom in 1446 AH (2025 CE) by:

Learning Roots Ltd.
Suite 15, Ideas House,
Eastwood Close,
London, E18 1BY,
United Kingdom

www.learningroots.com

Written by Zaheer Khatri, Dr. Azhar Majothi and Mariam Elgammal.
Layout and Illustrations by Fatima Zahur, Jannah Haque, Erika Gushiken, Daniela Montessi, Eduardo Estevão, Amanda Gomes, Oksana Potapova, Valery Uryvska, Kayla Olleres and Mariana Gutiez.

Acknowledgments
The publisher thanks Allāh, Lord of the worlds, for making this publication possible.

British Library Cataloguing in Publication Data
A CIP catalogue record for this book is available from the British Library.

Printed and bound in China
ISBN: 978-1-915381-13-2

LEARNING
ROOTS

MIRACLES
— OF THE —
Prophets عليهم السلام

Featuring

ZAYD
& FRIENDS

Contents

Publisher's Note

Young children are fascinated by things that are BIG and WOW. That explains why modern literature, movies, and toys for children gravitate toward concepts like magic, fairies, and giant beasts.

Yet, in Islam, we've been gifted with the perfect material for children: the Stories of the Prophets. These stories are not just for adults. They contain miracles, a fascinating layer of beauty for young children.

Miracles are not fables filled with fake magic or make-believe beasts. They're signs from Allah that actually happened. And that's one of the reasons why these stories are timeless. They stimulate minds, warm the hearts, and nourish the souls.

We believe this is the first book of its kind to focus on the miracles of the Prophets for young children and present them in a simple narrative supported by illustrations that tell the story.

This project required the combined efforts of all the talents at Learning Roots, making it our most collaborative endeavour yet. Every aspect, from concepts to text, images and design, was meticulously crafted to present the book you now hold in your hands.

We pray that Allah blesses you and your children with love and longing to be with His Prophets.

Zaheer Khatri & Yasmin Mussa
Founders of Learning Roots

Meet Zayd and Friends, your guides through the **Miracles of the Prophets.**

Zayd

Zayd loves to be with people and lead them with strong iman in doing good deeds.

Sarah

Sarah loves to explore the outdoors and play with animals and appreciate the great creations of Allah.

Yusuf

Yusuf loves adventure. He jumps at the chance to take part in any good project, especially ones that makes things better for people.

Nur

Nur loves finding the beauty in Allah's creation. She has a strong taste for good design and loves to work gently.

Deen

Deen is smart and loves reading, learning and thinking. The more he grows his mind, the more he appreciates the magnificent creations of Allah.

The Story of Adam عليه السلام

A long, long time ago,

Allah

created the
Heavens and Earth.

He also created **Angels**.

The Angels are
marvellous creatures
made of **light**.

They always do
what Allah says.

Allah told the Angels that He would make humans on Earth.

They would have the choice to do **right or wrong.**

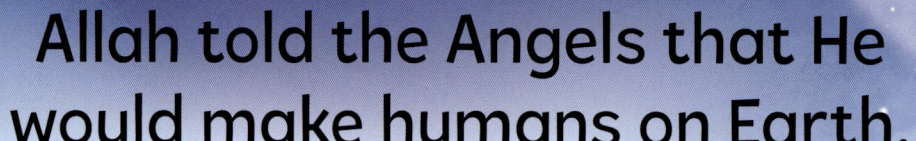

But the Angels were worried that humans would make a lot of trouble.

"I know something you don't know,"

Allah told the Angels.

Allah had a special plan.

In the Heavens,
Allah made Adam from

Clay

and

breathed **LIFE** into him.

Adam was the first human
to ever be created.

"Bow down to Adam,"

Allah told the Angels.

One by one,
all of the Angels
bowed to Adam
to show respect,

except
Shaytan!

Unlike the Angels,
he was a jinn.

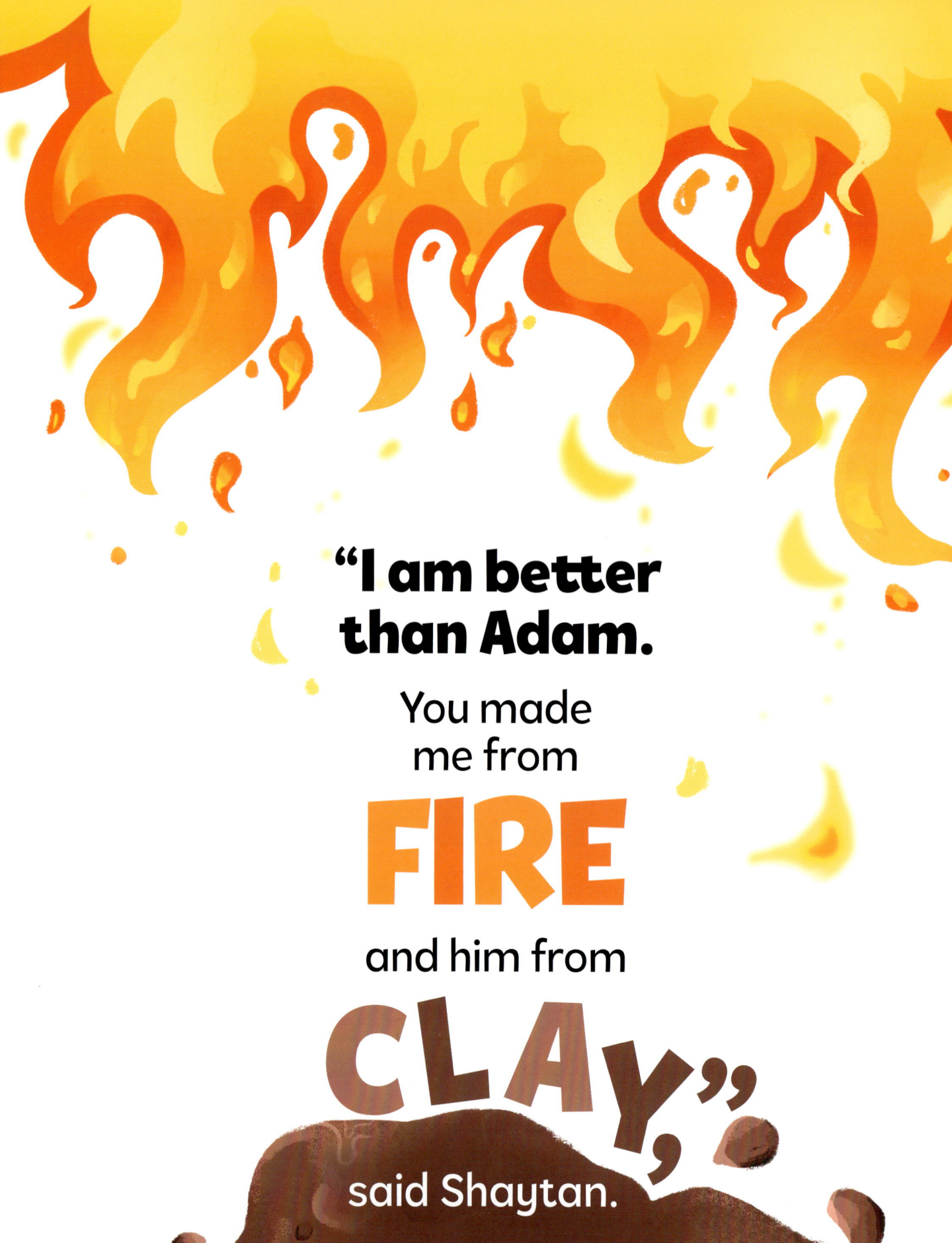

"I am better than Adam. You made me from **FIRE** and him from **CLAY,**" said Shaytan.

"LEAVE HERE!"

Allah ordered.

Shaytan was jealous and wanted Adam to leave the Heavens too.

Allah put Adam
a beautiful garden
called Jannah,

and made
a wife for him
called **Hawwa.**

"Eat from wherever you wish in Jannah, but **do not** 🚫 **go near this tree,"** said Allah.

This was the chance Shaytan was waiting for.

"If you eat from that tree, you will live forever,"

Shaytan kept on whissssspering to Adam and Hawwa.

Finally, Adam and Hawwa ate from the tree.

So Allah told them to leave Jannah and live on Earth.

But unlike Shaytan, they realised they had made a

BIG mistake.

"**O Allah**
...If You don't forgive us and have mercy on us, we will be lost!" Adam and Hawwa said to Allah.

Allah forgave them because He is the Most Kind.

Now, Shaytan was even more jealous.

He promised to keep **whisssssspering** bad ideas to Adam's children.

But to help us against Shaytan, Allah sent Prophets with **MIRACLES** to guide us to Jannah.

The Story of Nuh عليه السلام

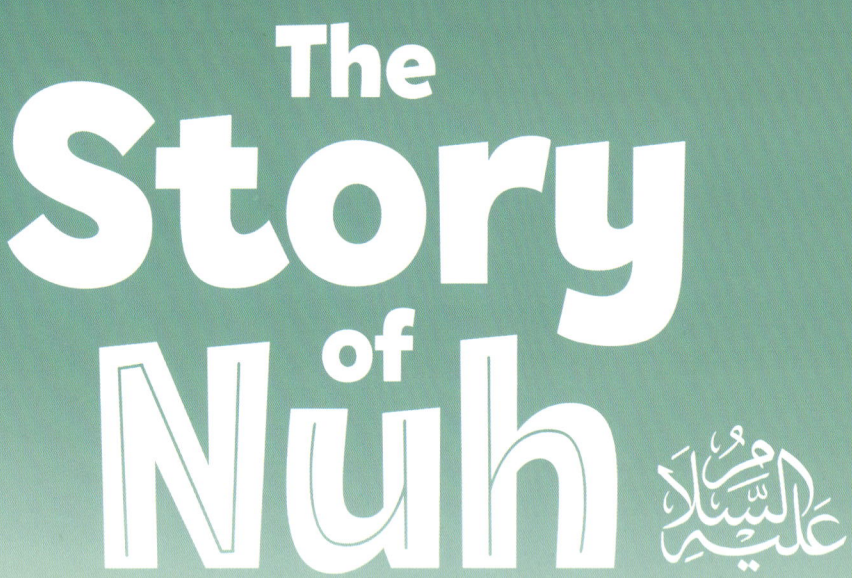

After Prophet Adam passed away, Shaytan tricked people into praying to idols.

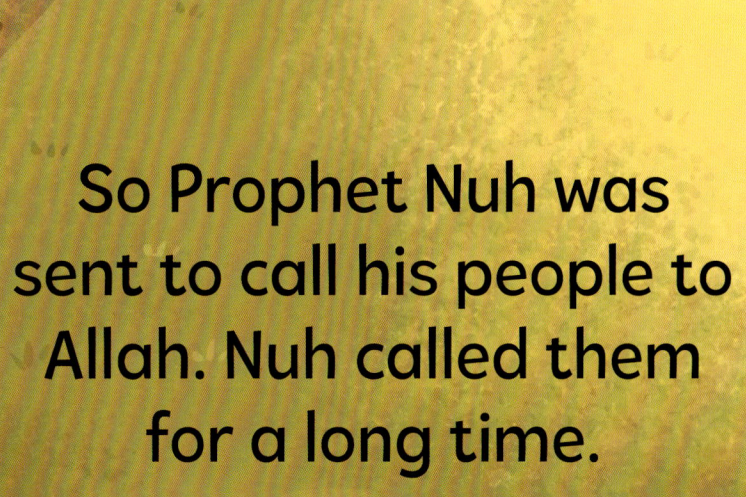

So Prophet Nuh was sent to call his people to Allah. Nuh called them for a long time.

Not for a **DAY.**

Not for a **WEEK.**

Not even for a **YEAR.**

But for hundreds of years!

A few people believed Nuh.
But most people
ignored his message.

Then one day,
Allah
told Nuh to

...start building

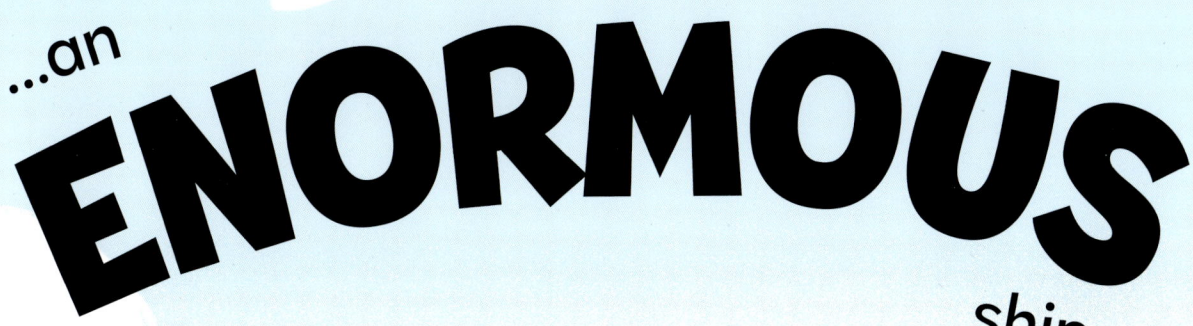

...an **ENORMOUS** ship.

Nuh worked very hard, chopping trees and hammering nails.

The ship had to be **very strong.**

Some people who didn't believe in Allah, teased Nuh.

HA!

HA!

HA!

"So you're a carpenter now?" they chuckled.

But Nuh kept on building.

"Have you gone crazy?" they sniggered.

But Nuh kept on **building.**

"That's a big ship for one man!" they mocked.

But Nuh kept on **building.**

The ship was finally ready.

But Nuh still had one more thing to do.

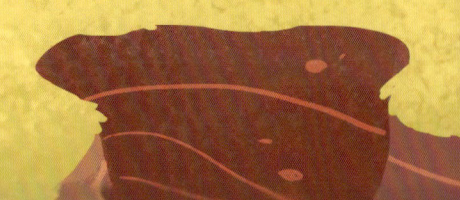

Allah told
him to bring

**pairs of
animals**

onto the ship.

All kinds of animals climbed on board.

What a sight it was!

The ship was crowded with animals,

HUGE

and tiny,

...scaly and furry,
spotted and stripy.

Prophet Nuh,
his followers
and the animals
were ready to sail.

But on what?

RUMMMMMBLE...

The ground suddenly Shook!

Water **BURST** out
of the ground.

And **heavy rain** poured
from the sky.

Oh no! There was a GIGANTIC FLOOD!

But Nuh was not worried. **"Bismillah,** with Allah's help we sail," he said.

The storm suddenly stopped
and the water drained away.
The ship rested

on **top** of a

mountain.

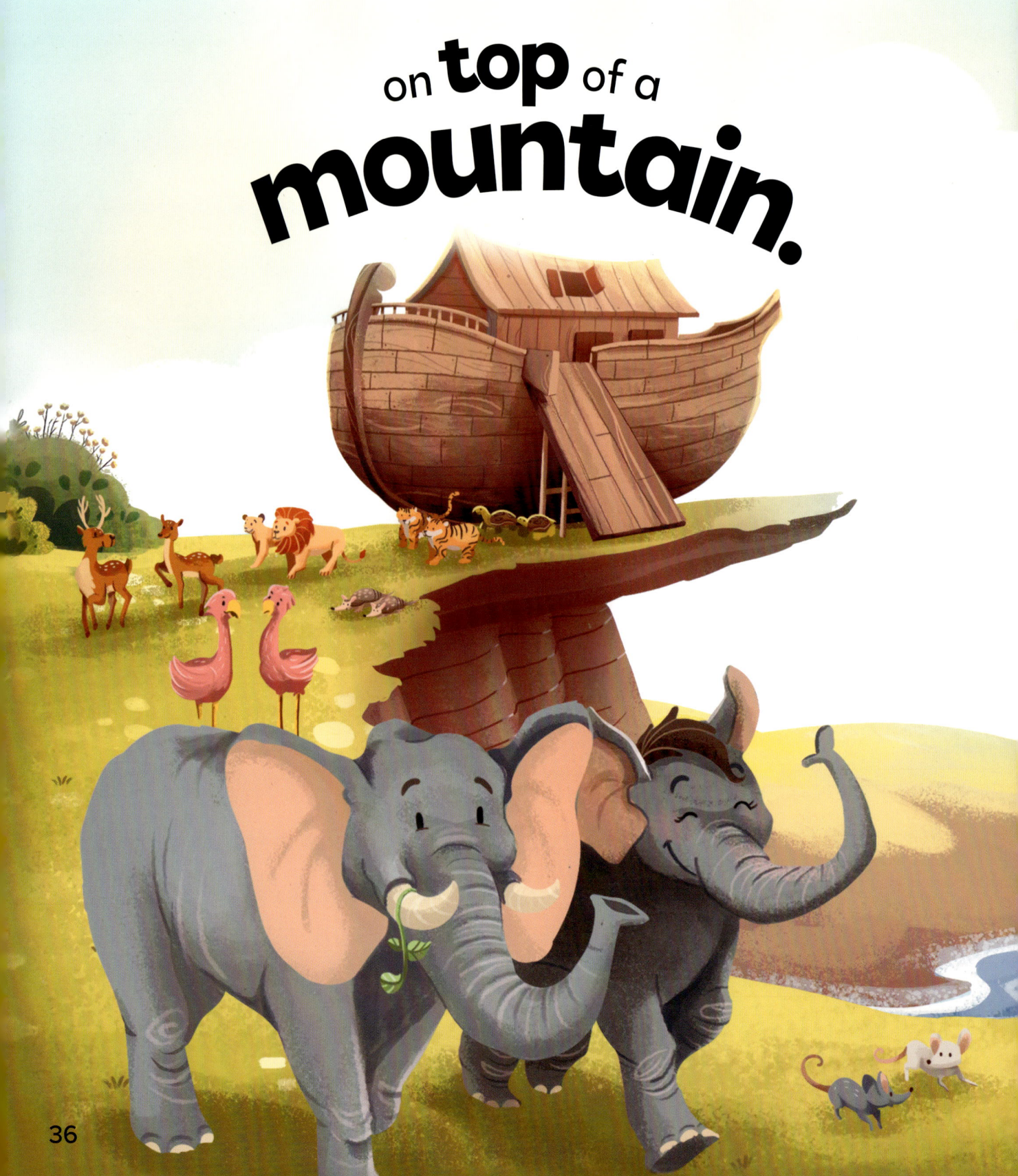

Everyone had
been washed away
by the flood, except
Prophet Nuh,
his followers
and the animals.

It was a
MIRACLE
from **Allah.**

The Story of Saleh عليه السلام

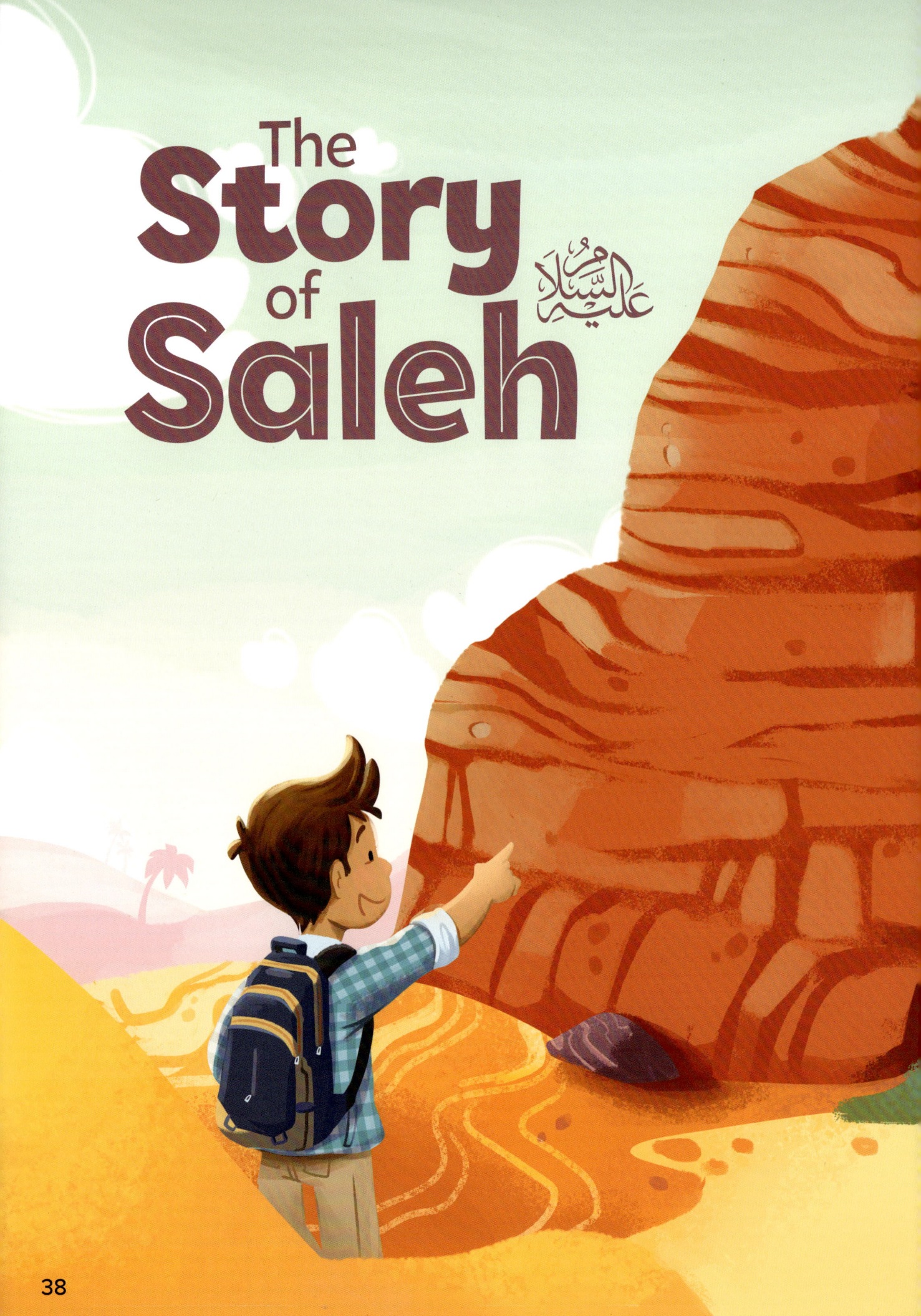

Prophet Saleh lived in a
town called al-Hijr
with the tribe of Thamud.

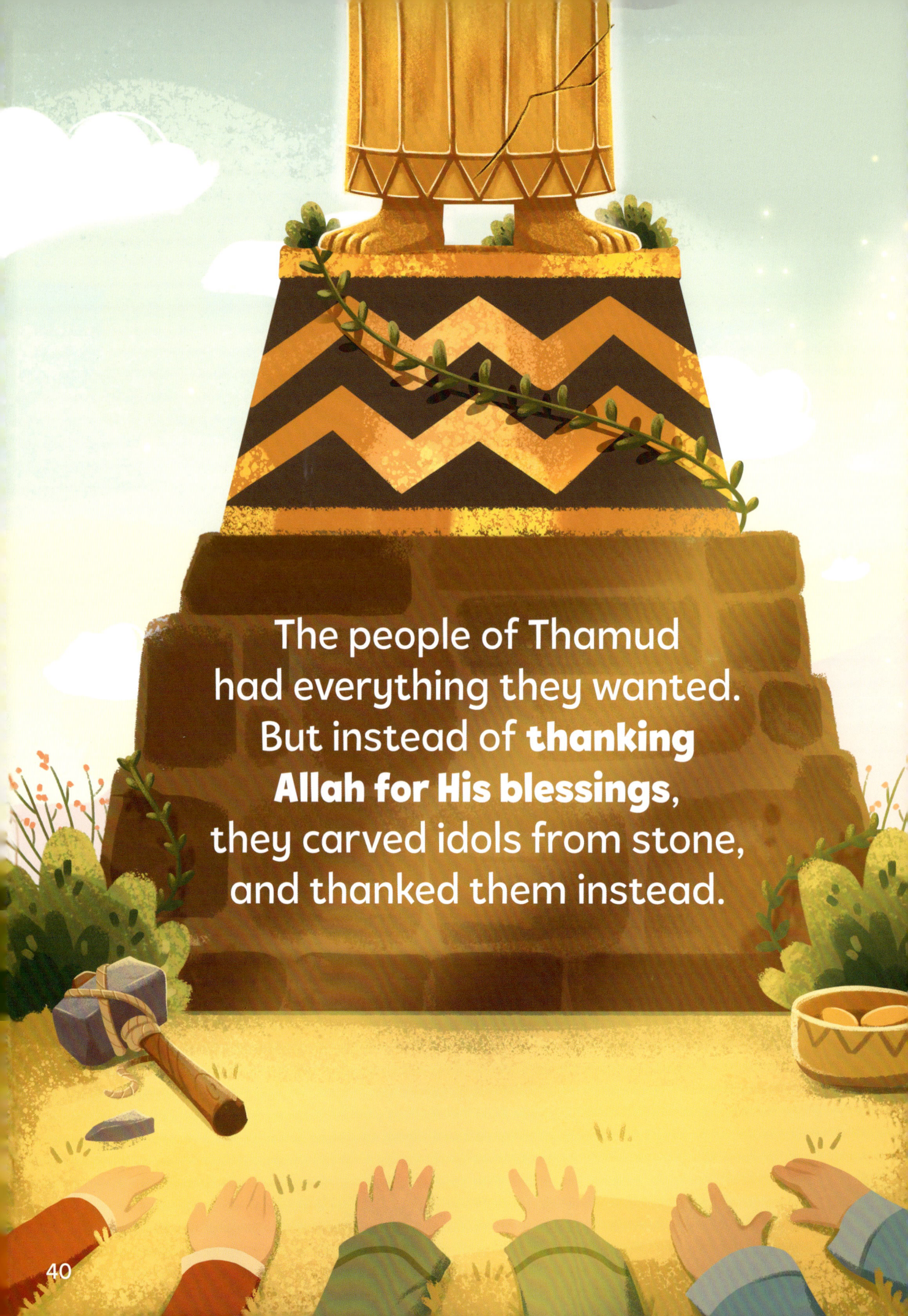

The people of Thamud
had everything they wanted.
But instead of **thanking
Allah for His blessings**,
they carved idols from stone,
and thanked them instead.

"O my people,"
said Saleh,

"There is only One True God, Allah.

Pray to,
ask
and thank **HIM.**

Your idols cannot help you.
They cannot even hear you."

Some people followed Saleh.

But there were others,
who didn't believe
anything he said.

"Show us a sign!"
they shouted.

Ha Ha Ha Ha

If you show us a miracle,
then we'll believe you!"

Saleh placed his **trust in Allah.**

He raised his hands towards the sky and prayed for a splendid sign.

Soon the Earth

trembled.

Was it an earthquake?
Or a screeching storm?
Not quite…

"It's coming from up there!"

shouted a man from the crowd.

Everyone looked at the mountain.

Suddenly, there was a **LOUD** CRACK!

An **ENORMOUS rock** tumbled down to the ground.

Out came a

BIG

camel!

It was a
MIRACLE
from **Allah.**

"**This is a sign from Allah!**"

Saleh said to his people.

"Be kind to this special camel and share your water with her."

"We believe in Allah!"

called out a group from the crowd.

Saleh was happy to see more people believing in Allah.

But most of the people were grumpy and still did not believe Saleh.

"Share **OUR** water with the camel?"

"**NO WAY!**" shouted the grumpy bunch.

"Remember, the camel is a sign from Allah. So do not harm her in any way," said Saleh.

But the grumpy bunch didn't listen.

"Enough is enough!"

they finally decided.

"People have left our idols.
And the camel is drinking our water.

We've got to get rid of it!"

And so they made
an evil plan.

They crept up
to the camel
at night.

When the grumpy bunch
got close enough,
they hit the camel!

The camel screamed in pain.
Its loud cry woke up
the people of al-Hijr.

The grumpy brunch ran away.

Saleh and his followers
hurried towards the sound.
They found the camel.

Sadly, it had died.

How could people
do such an evil thing?

Allah told Saleh to warn
his people.

They had
three days
to ask for
forgiveness,
otherwise...

...they would get a
terrible
punishment.

But they
didn't care.

3 DAYS PASSED.

A **howling** wind
ripped through the town.

whoo°O

oosh!

It sent people
flying left and right...

and shook the ground.

The people of Thamud were

NO MORE.

But Allah saved
Prophet Saleh
and his followers.

Allah

always protects the believers.

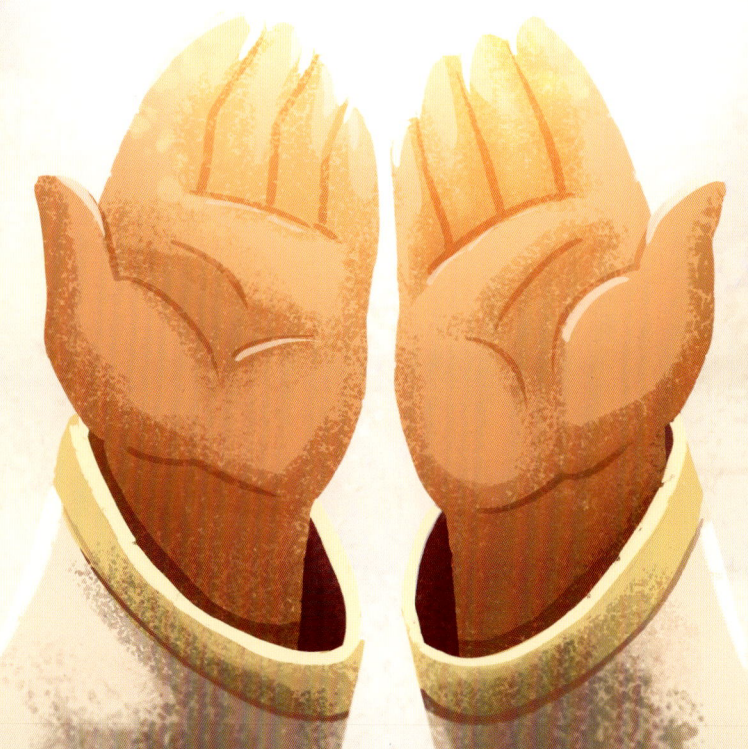

The Story of Ibrahim عليه السلام

In a land called Babylon, everyone worshipped idols at the temple.

Except for a very special, young man named Ibrahim. He knew that only Allah can help and protect us.

Prophet Ibrahim told his people to pray to Allah alone.

But they did not listen.

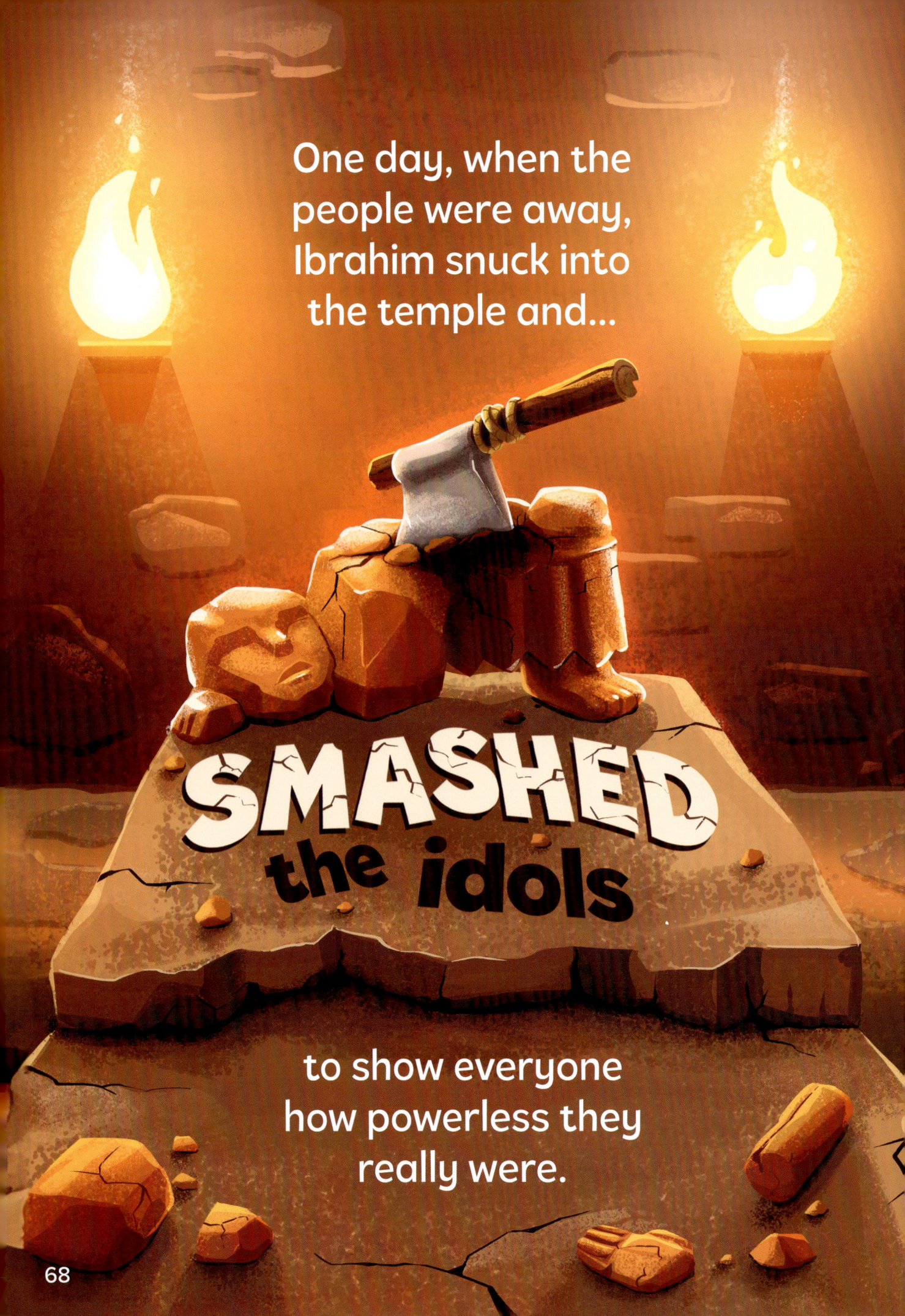

One day, when the people were away, Ibrahim snuck into the temple and...

SMASHED the idols

to show everyone how powerless they really were.

"Who did that to **OUR GODS?**"

the people asked each other.

"It must have been Ibrahim. **GET HIM!**"

they said.

They took Ibrahim
to the King of Babylon.
The king ordered his men to light

the
**biggest,
hottest
FIRE**
anyone had ever seen.

Then the king told them
to build a **GIANT** catapult
and throw Ibrahim into the fire.

**"Allah is all I need.
He is the
best Protector,"**
whispered Ibrahim
as he was sent flying
into the raging fire.

"O fire!
Be cool and safe
for Ibrahim!"
Allah ordered.

Ibrahim walked out
of the fire without
a single burn.

It was a
MIRACLE
from Allah.

The people of Babylon still did not believe Ibrahim.

So he left in search of a new place where he could raise a family of believers.

The Story of Ismail  عليه السلام

Prophet Ibrahim and his wife Hajar had a baby boy called Ismail.

One day,
Allah gave Ibrahim a
special message.

He had to take Hajar
and baby Ismail
on a very long trip.

In a hot, stoney place called Makkah, where there were no trees or water, Ibrahim stopped his camel.

He helped Hajar and Ismail down.

Ibrahim turned to leave.
Hajar panicked and asked,

"Has Allah asked you to do this?"

"Yes," Ibrahim replied.

"Then Allah will look after us," said Hajar.

As Ibrahim rode away,
he prayed to Allah
to bless Hajar and Ismail
in the land of Makkah.

The food and drink was

running out...

Hajar held her baby and prayed to Allah.

Hajar thought she might find help on two nearby hills. They were called...

SAFA and

She ran as fast as she could,

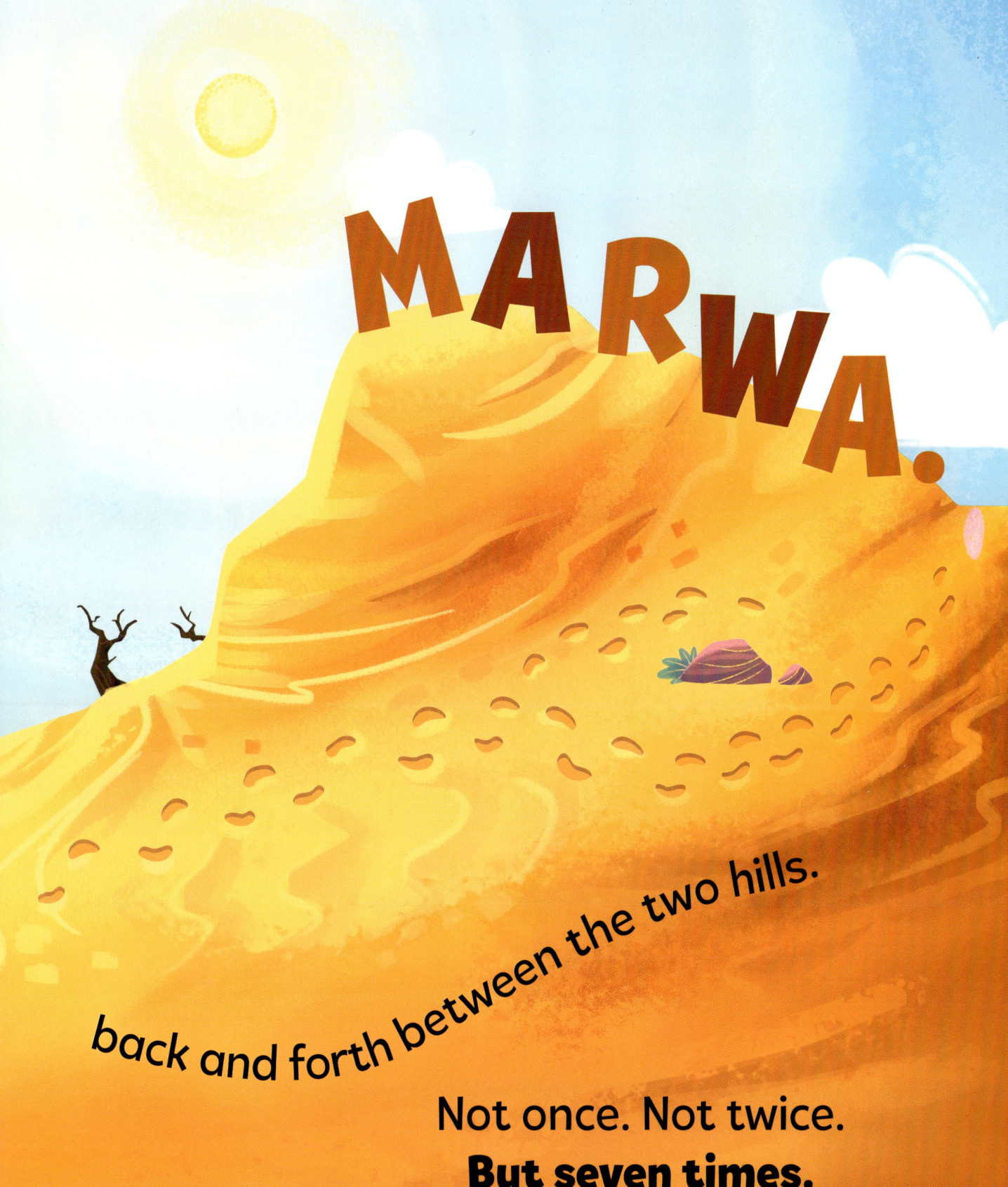

MARWA.

back and forth between the two hills.

Not once. Not twice.
But seven times.
There was no one in sight.

Just then, Hajar heard a noise.
She hurried back to Ismail.

GASP!

She saw an Angel digging
the ground with its wing.

**Water suddenly
spouted out.**

The water was called **Zam zam** and it **flowed** and **flowed.**

Many years later,
Ibrahim returned to Makkah.

Ismail became a
Prophet of Allah,
just like his father.

Together, they built the

Ka'bah,

a place to pray to
Allah alone.

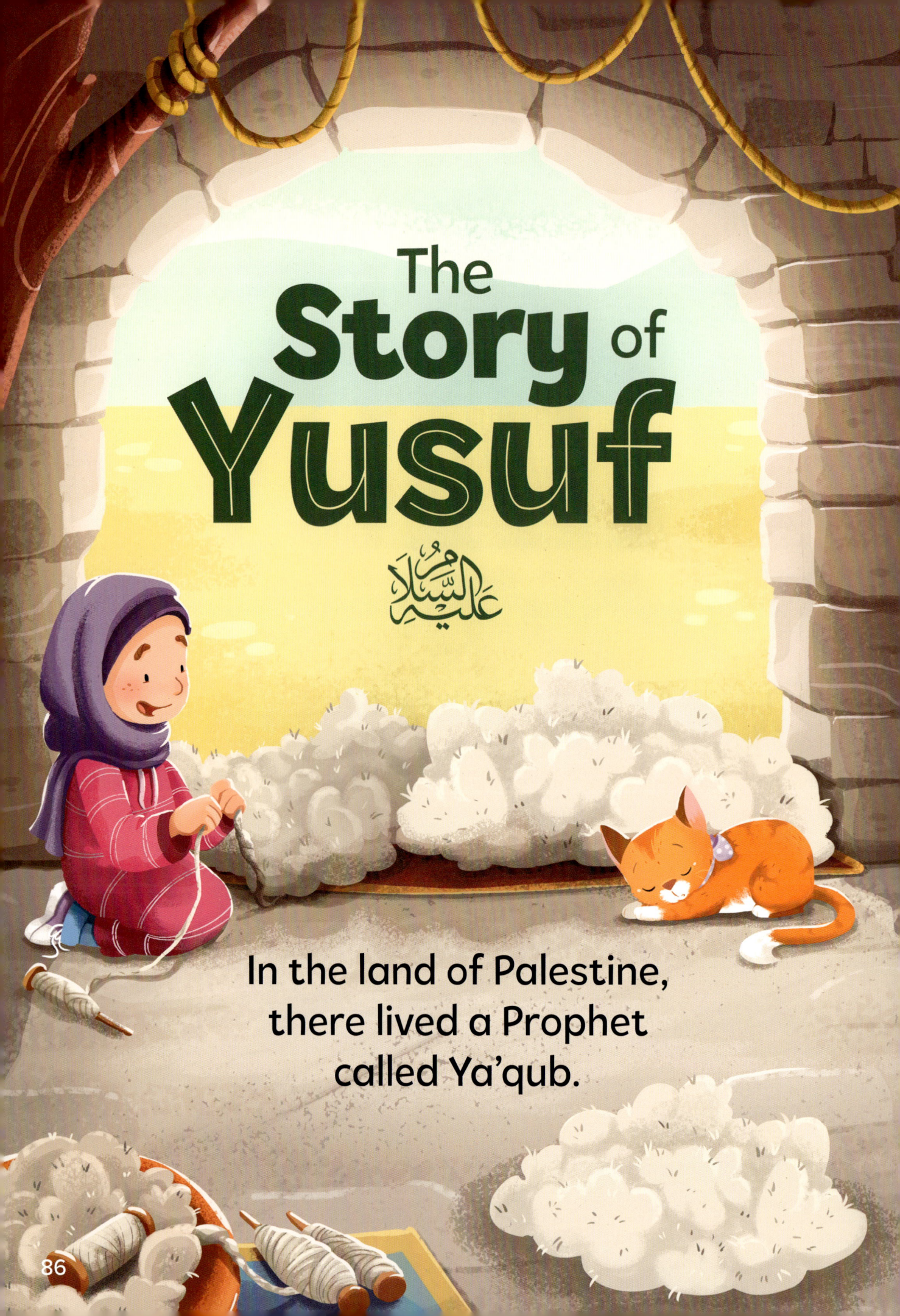

The Story of Yusuf

عَلَيْهِ السَّلَام

In the land of Palestine, there lived a Prophet called Ya'qub.

He had
12 strong sons.
His favourite son
was a sweet boy
called Yusuf.

One day,
Yusuf said to
his father,

"In my dream
I saw the sun,
the moon, and
11 stars bowing
down to me!"

"Don't tell your brothers about your dream," said Ya'qub.

They might plan to hurt you."

And that's exactly what they did.

"Father loves Yusuf more than us," said the brothers.

"Let's throw Yusuf into a well!"

The brothers took
Yusuf into the fields.
And just as
they planned,

they threw Yusuf down a WELL.

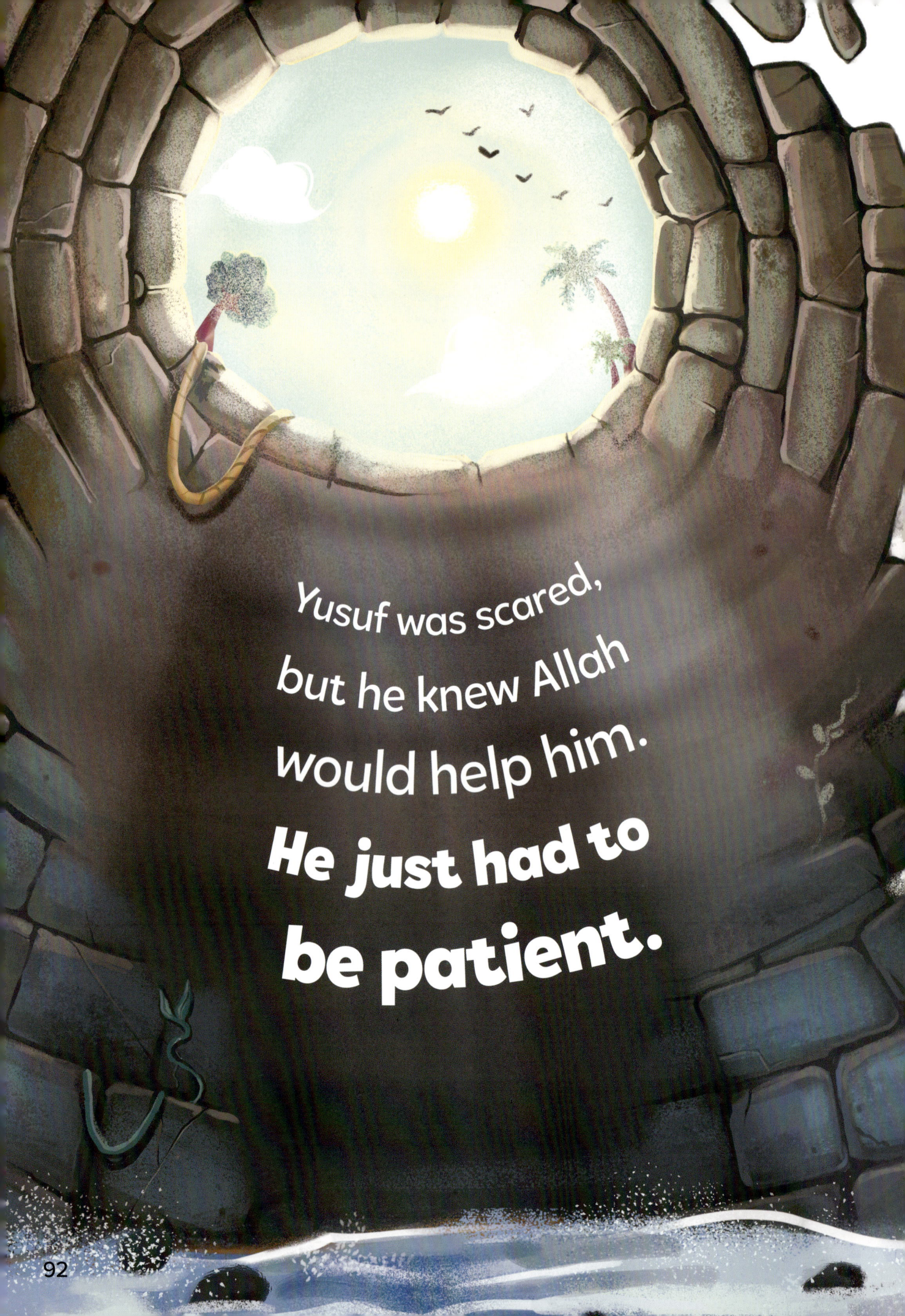

Yusuf was scared, but he knew Allah would help him. **He just had to be patient.**

When the brothers returned
home, they told Ya'qub that
a wolf had eaten Yusuf.

But Ya'qub knew
they were lying.

He just had to
be patient.

A group of
travellers passed
by the well.

They picked Yusuf up
and took him to a
faraway land called
Egypt.

When Yusuf grew up,
the king of Egypt
chose him to look after
the kingdom's food.

Yusuf was smart
and saved some food
every year.

Back in Palestine,
there was no rain.
Ya'qub and his family
ran out of food.

Ya'qub sent
his sons to
get food
from Egypt.

"Yes! I am Yusuf. **Allah looked after me.** Bring the rest of our family here," he said to his brothers.

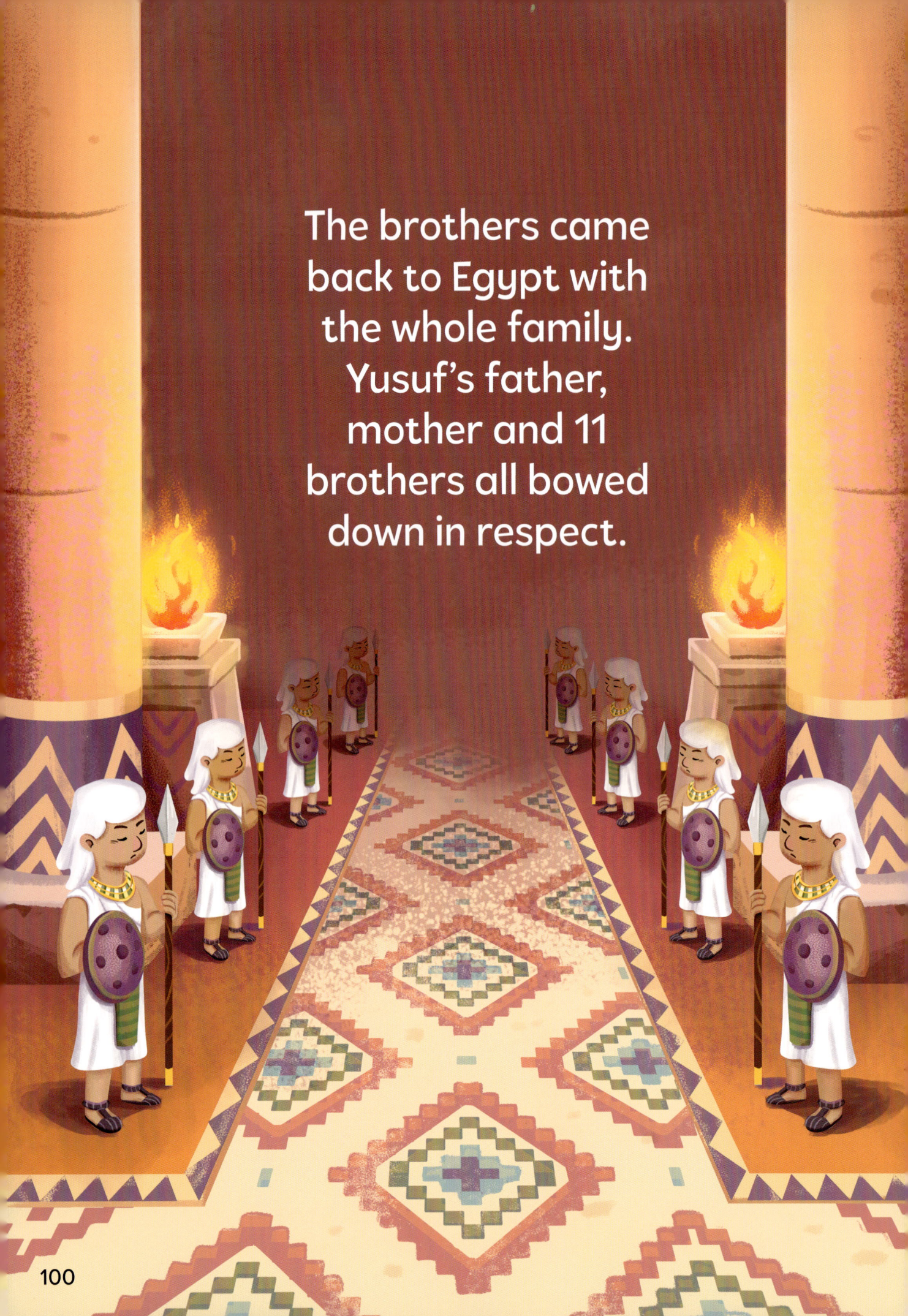

The brothers came back to Egypt with the whole family. Yusuf's father, mother and 11 brothers all bowed down in respect.

Yusuf remembered
his dream of the sun,
the moon and 11 stars.

"Father!
**My dream has
come true!"**
said Yusuf.

It was a
MIRACLE
from **Allah.**

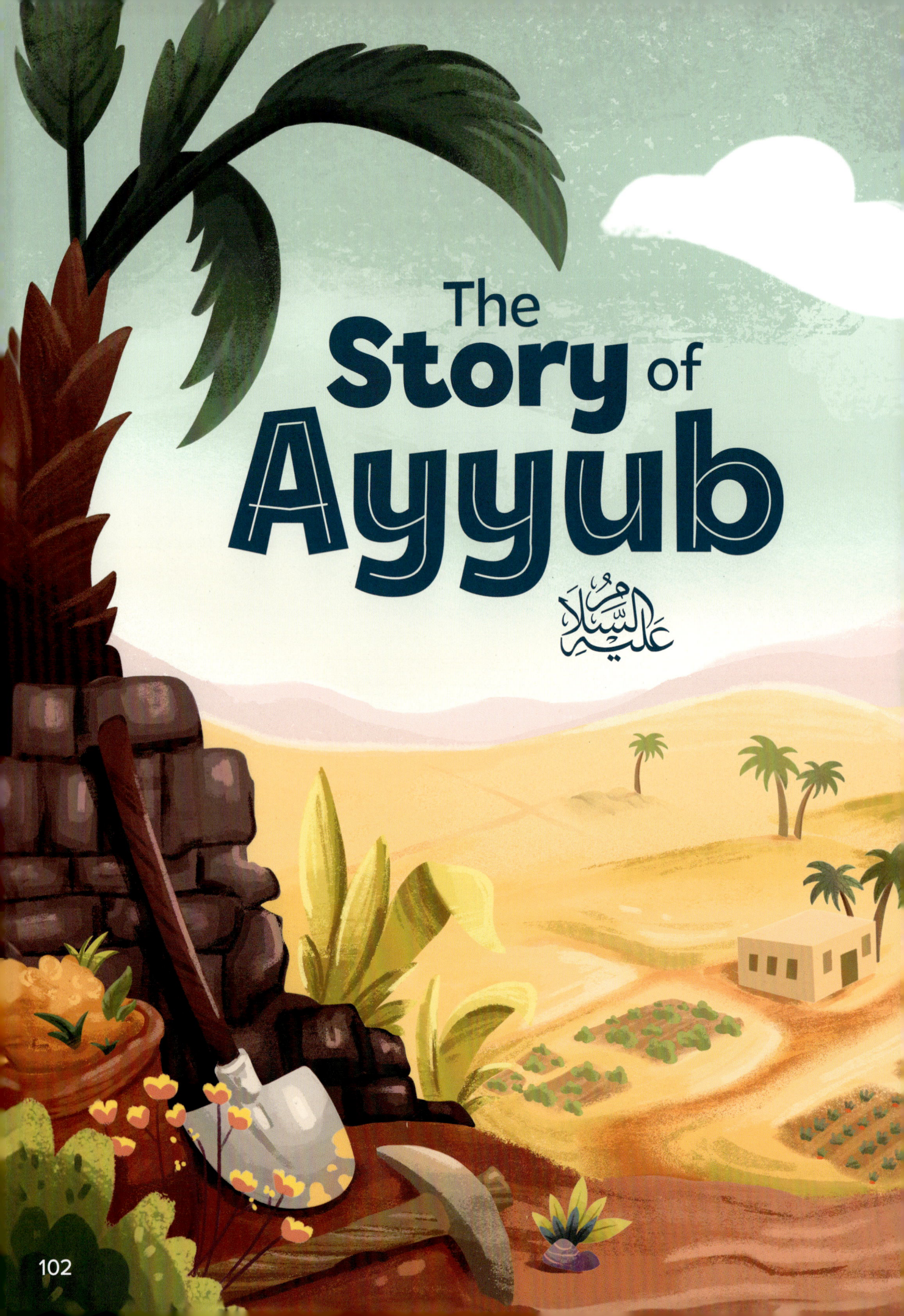

The Story of Ayyub عليه السلام

Prophet Ayyub
lived on a farm.

The farm had
rows and rows of
juicy fruits

and
vegetables.

Fluffy sheep grazed next to happy cows,

and playful chicks chased after clucking hens.

Ayyub had a big family too, with lots of children.

They all helped him take care of the farm.

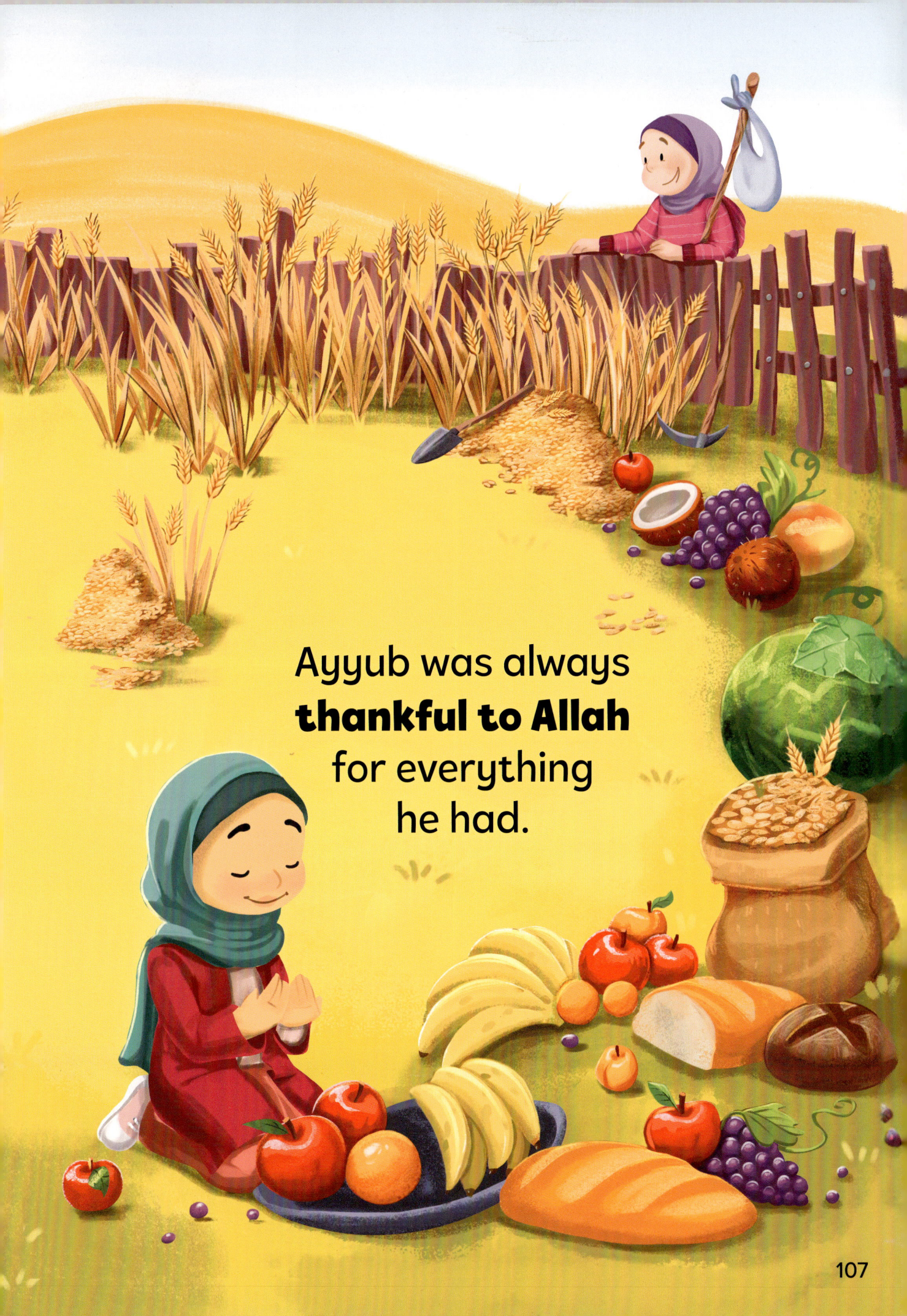

Ayyub was always **thankful to Allah** for everything he had.

One morning,

DISASTER STRUCK.

All the plants died.

The animals became thin.

Ayyub felt
weak and **achy.**

Then, things got
harder...

Ayyub lost
his children.
His helpers left
the farm and
his neighbours
stayed away.

Then, things got even
harder...

Ayyub fell so ill
that he couldn't get
out of bed anymore.

But he was
always thankful
and made dua
to Allah.

"I am in a lot of pain, but You are the **Most Merciful.**"

Just then, Allah sent
a special message.

"**Stamp**
your **foot!**
Here is cool water for
you to drink and wash."

As soon as Ayyub drank
the water, his illness
went away...

Then, things got even
better...

Allah gave Ayyub
his farm back.

It was even

BIGGER

than before!

Next, Allah gave him all
of his children back,
along with even more.

Ayyub was
always patient
and thankful.

It was a
MIRACLE
from **Allah.**

The Story of Yunus عليه السلام

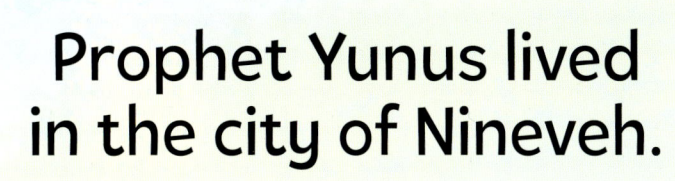

Prophet Yunus lived
in the city of Nineveh.

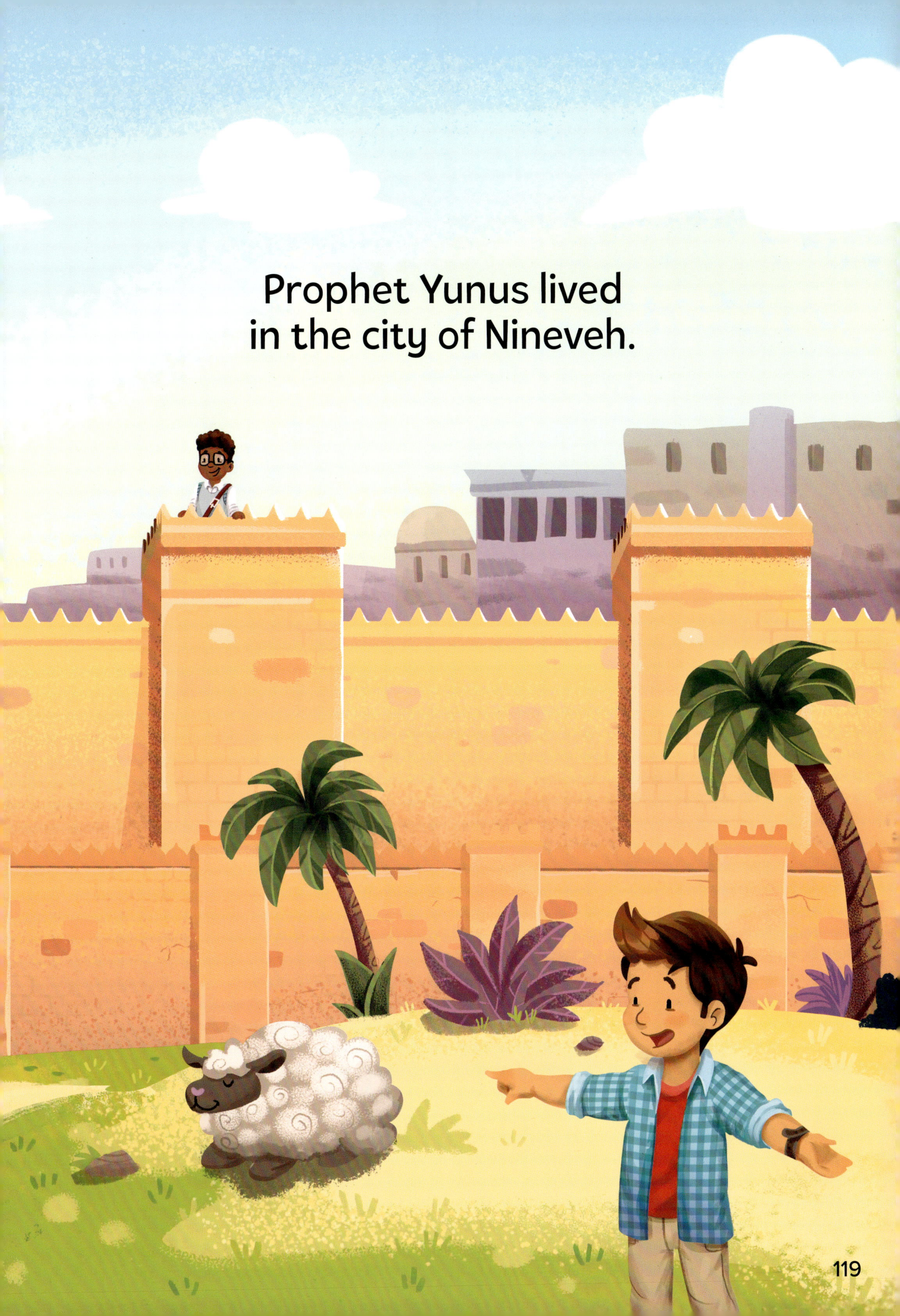

The people in the city prayed to idols.

Yunus told them to **pray to Allah alone.**

But the people didn't listen.

So, Yunus decided it
was time to leave Nineveh.

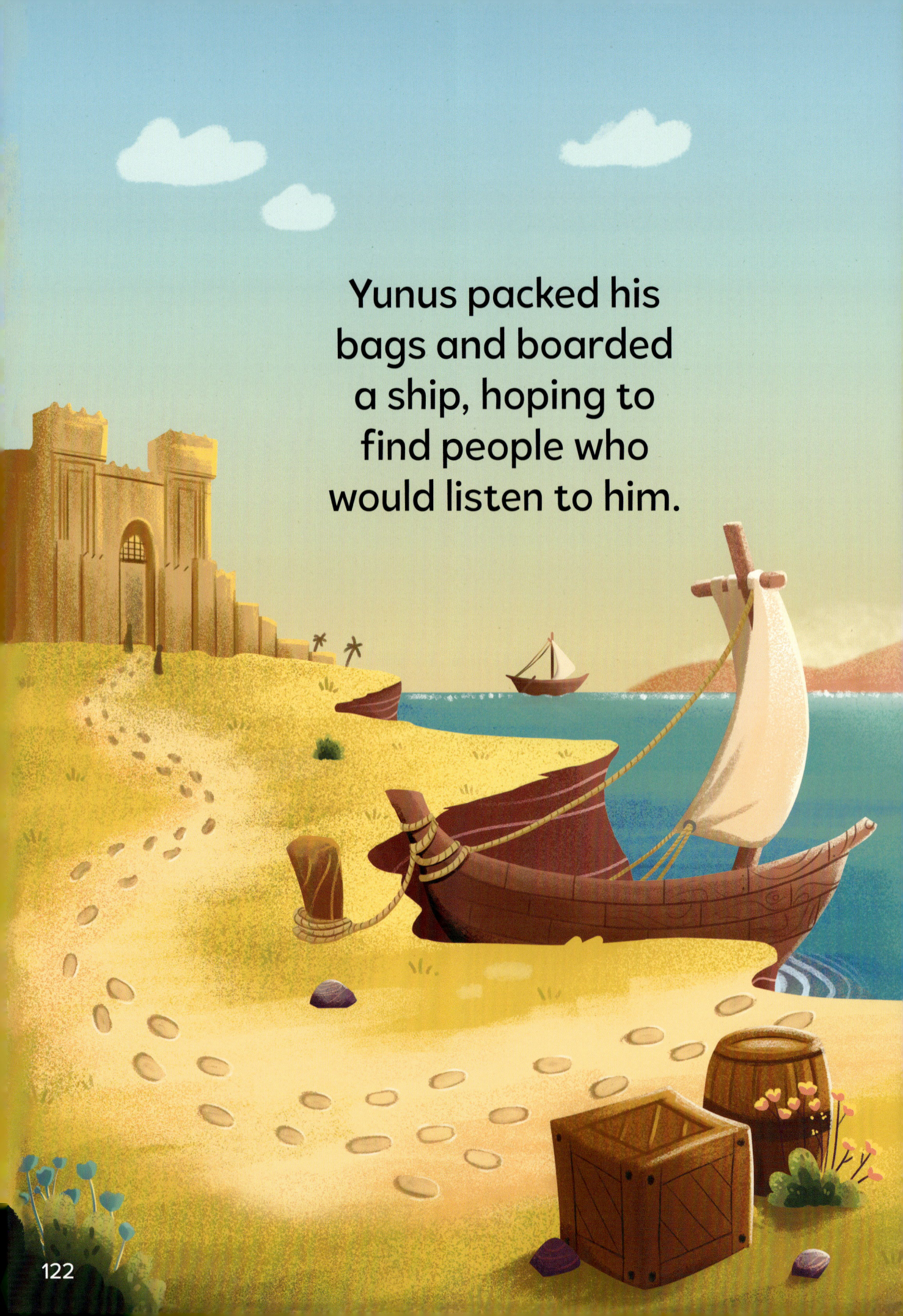

Yunus packed his bags and boarded a ship, hoping to find people who would listen to him.

But Allah did not tell him to leave Nineveh.

A HUGE STORM

struck the sea.

Water **splashed** onto the deck.

The ship rocked from **side** to **side.**

The sailors threw their bags into the sea to make the ship lighter.

But nothing helped.

The sailors wrote everyone's names on

to decide who to throw overboard.

Every time
they picked a stick,
the same name
came up...

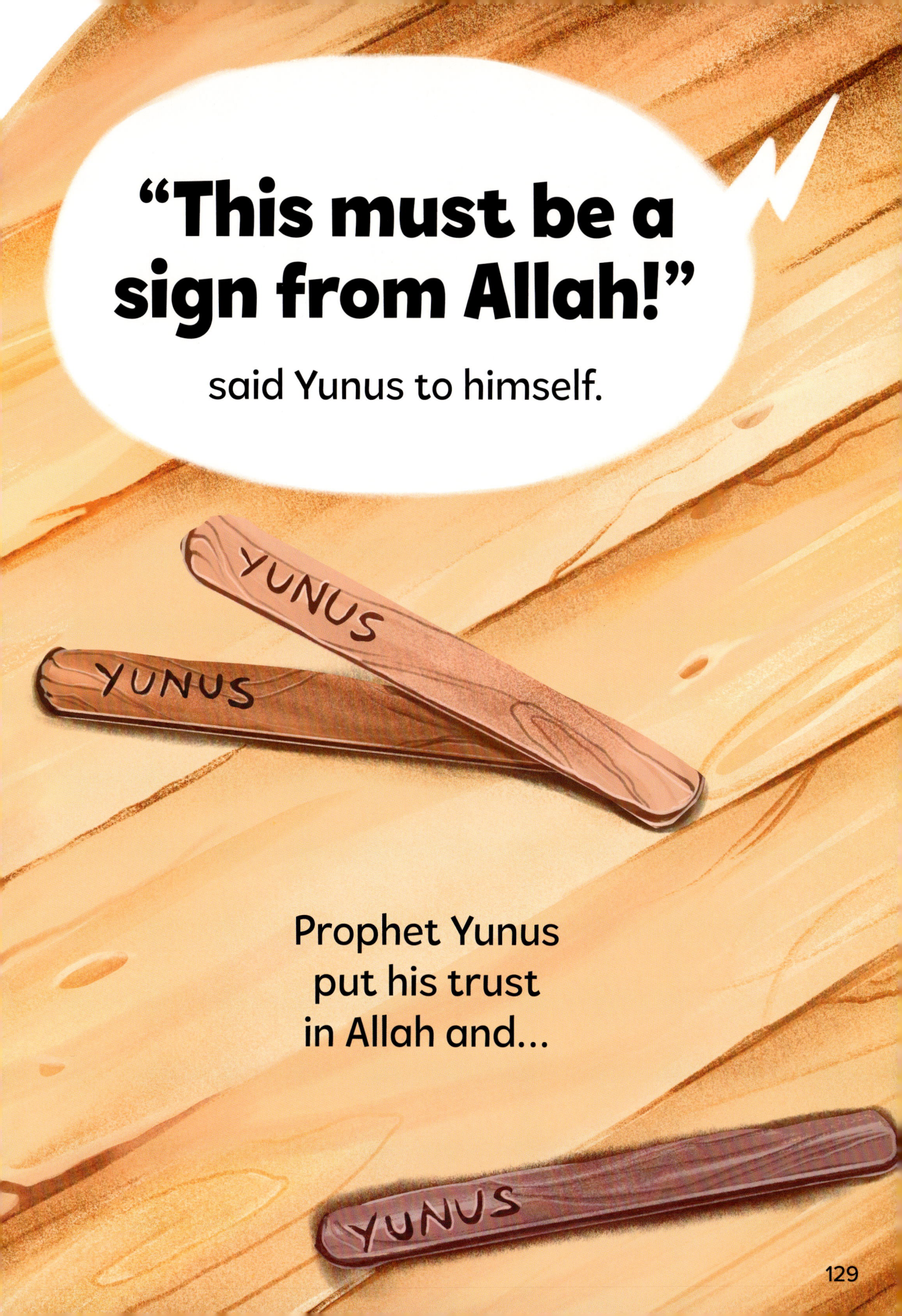

"**This must be a sign from Allah!**"

said Yunus to himself.

Prophet Yunus put his trust in Allah and...

...jumped into
the sea.

HE SANK
into the dark water.

It got darker

and darker.

Suddenly he couldn't see anything.

Yunus realised
he was inside a
SLIMY,
GOOEY,
SMELLY
belly of a
GIANT
WHALE!

There was
no way out.
So Yunus made
dua to Allah.

"Allah!
There is no
God but You.
How perfect You are.
I made a mistake."

133

Allah answered
Yunus' dua.
The whale opened
its mouth and
Yunus escaped.

He swam back to
dry land, thankful
for Allah's help.

Yunus returned to Nineveh
to continue calling his
people to Allah.

To his surprise,
his people now
believed in Allah and
prayed to Him alone!

It was a
MIRACLE
from **Allah.**

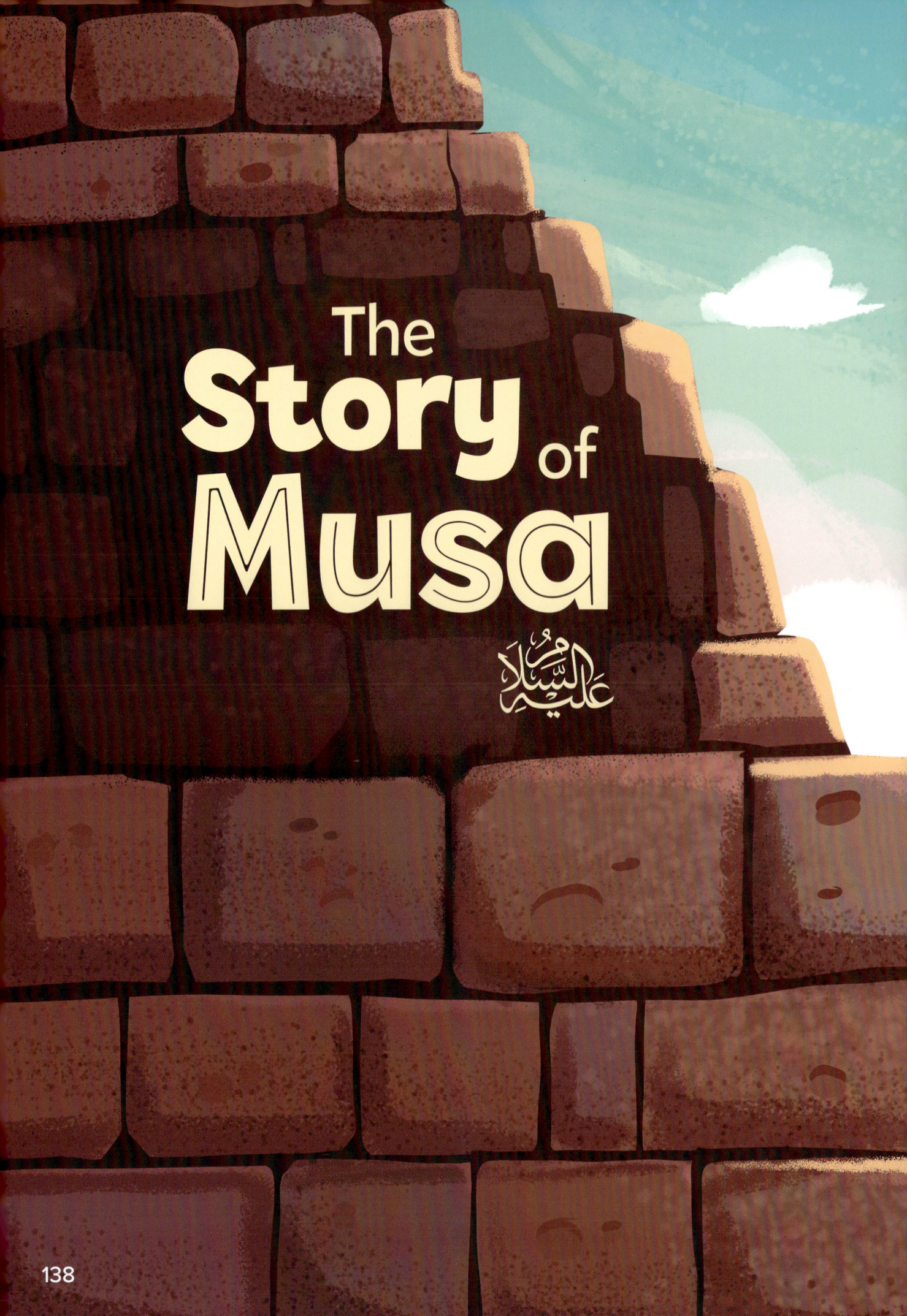

The Story of Musa عليه السلام

In the land of Egypt,
there lived two
groups of people,
the Egyptians and
the Israelites.

139

Egypt was ruled by an evil king called **Pharaoh.**

He was especially **nasty** to the Israelites, who were from the family of Ya'qub.

Baby Musa
was from
the Israelites.

Musa's mother
was scared that
Pharaoh would
hurt her
baby boy.

Allah told her
to put Musa in a

basket

and place it in the river.

The wife of Pharaoh picked up the basket. She was a kind lady and looked for someone to care for the baby.

She picked…
Musa's mother!

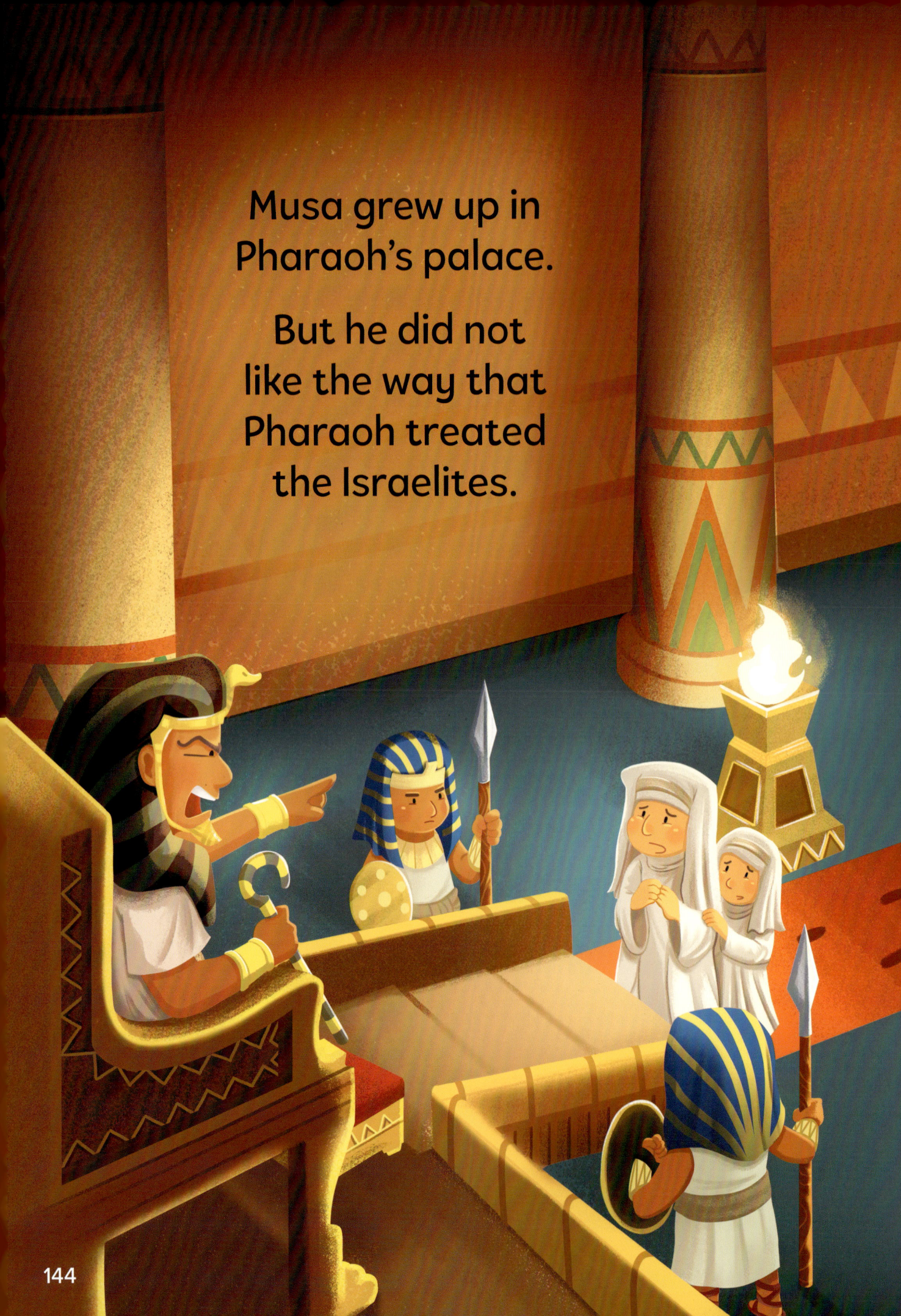

Musa grew up in Pharaoh's palace.

But he did not like the way that Pharaoh treated the Israelites.

Even worse than that, Pharaoh said he was God!

So Musa decided to leave Egypt.

One day, Musa was
walking up a special

mountain and
heard a voice,

"O Musa!
I am Allah.
There is no
God but Me."

Allah made Musa
a Prophet and gave
him some miracles.
"Go to Pharaoh, and show
him My signs," Allah said.

So Musa returned to Egypt.

Musa told Pharaoh
about Allah, but Pharaoh
became angry.

Musa pulled out his hand from his pocket and showed Pharoah one of the miracles.

Musa's hand glowed white.

But Pharaoh thought it was magic. So he gathered his best magicians to face Musa.

Everyone in Egypt came to
see the show.

The magicians threw ropes
and sticks on the ground and
turned them into snakes,

wiggling

from here to there.

But it was just a magic trick.

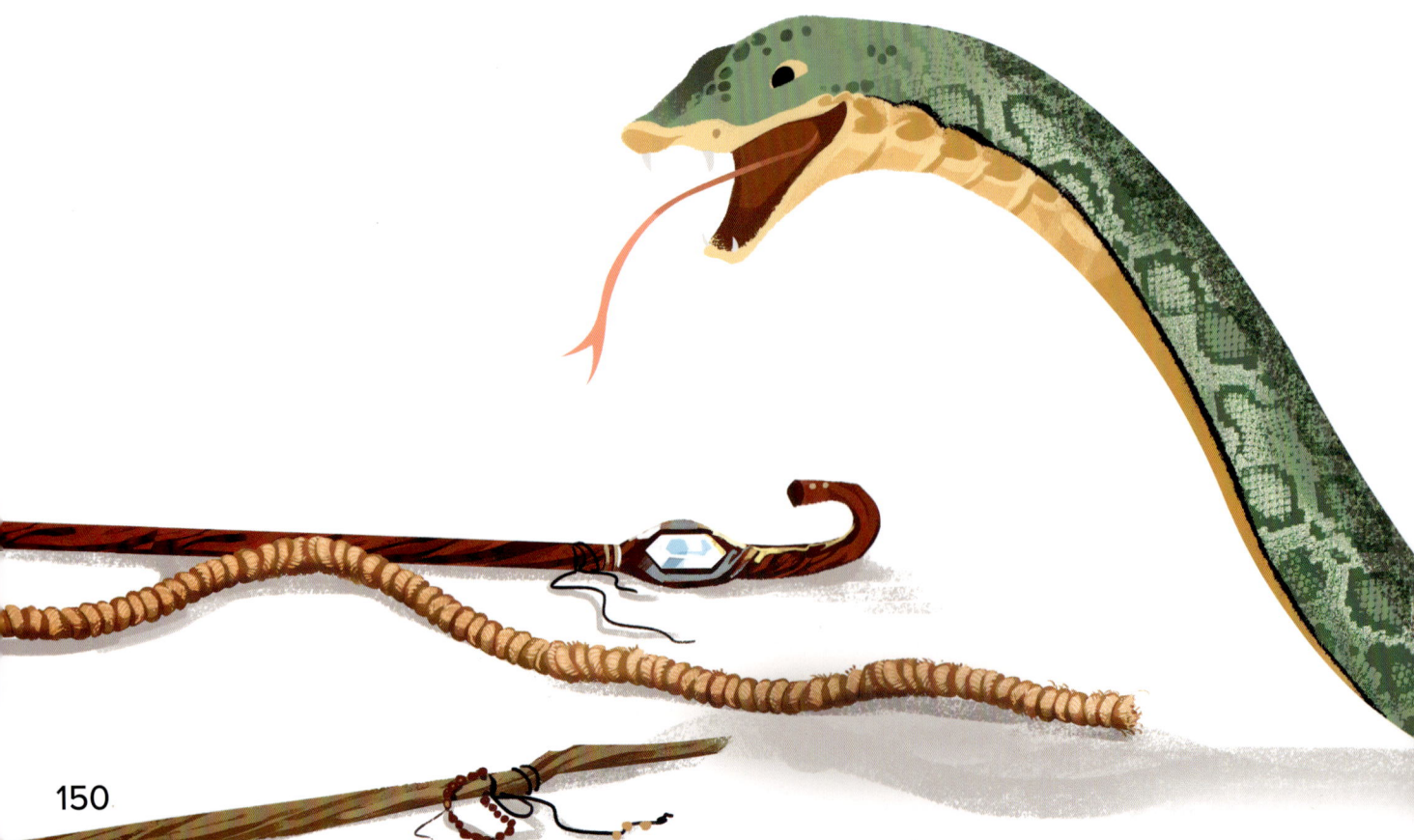

Now it was Musa's turn.
He threw his stick and
it turned into a
real snake. It gobbled up
all the other snakes there.

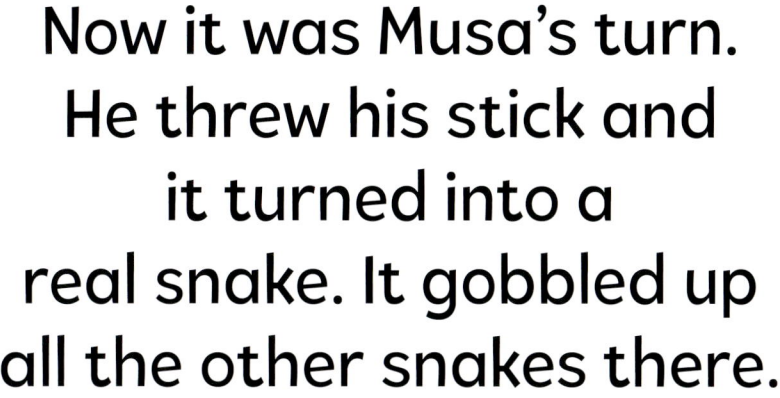

The magicians knew this was
a miracle and not magic.

Pharoah become
even more angry. He decided to
punish Musa, the magicians
and the Israelites.

So Allah told Musa
to leave Egypt
with his followers.

But Pharaoh gathered
his army and chased
after them.

Musa and his followers
ran as fast as they could until
they reached the sea.

They could not find a way
across and Pharaoh was
catching up fast.

"Oh no! Pharaoh's army
will soon catch us!"
said Musa's followers.

"No way!"

said Musa,
"Allah is with me and He
will show us a way out!"

"O Musa! Strike the sea with your stick,"

Allah ordered.

And as soon as Musa did...

Musa and
his followers
crossed to
the other side
of the sea.

Pharaoh and
his army
**charged
forward.**

But Allah made the sea cave in. Pharaoh and his army DROWNED.

160

Musa and his followers were safe.

It was a
MIRACLE
from **Allah.**

The Story of Dawud  عليه السلام

In the city of Jerusalem,
there lived a brave king
called Talut.

King Talut marched out of Jerusalem with his army to defend the city from...

GIANT JALUT!

It was scorching hot and the army passed by a river.

"Whoever drinks
from this river cannot
come with me,"
said King Talut.

Most of the soldiers drank
from the river, except for
a few, including a young
man called...

Dawud.

He listened to the king
and did not go near
the river.

King Talut ordered
the soldiers who drank from
the river to go back
to Jerusalem.

With less men, but
more patience, the army
marched on.

They came face-to-face
with **GIANT JALUT** and his
mighty army.

Everyone was scared
to fight him.

"Who will be brave
enough to fight
Giant Jalut?"
King Talut asked.

**Dawud stepped
forward.**

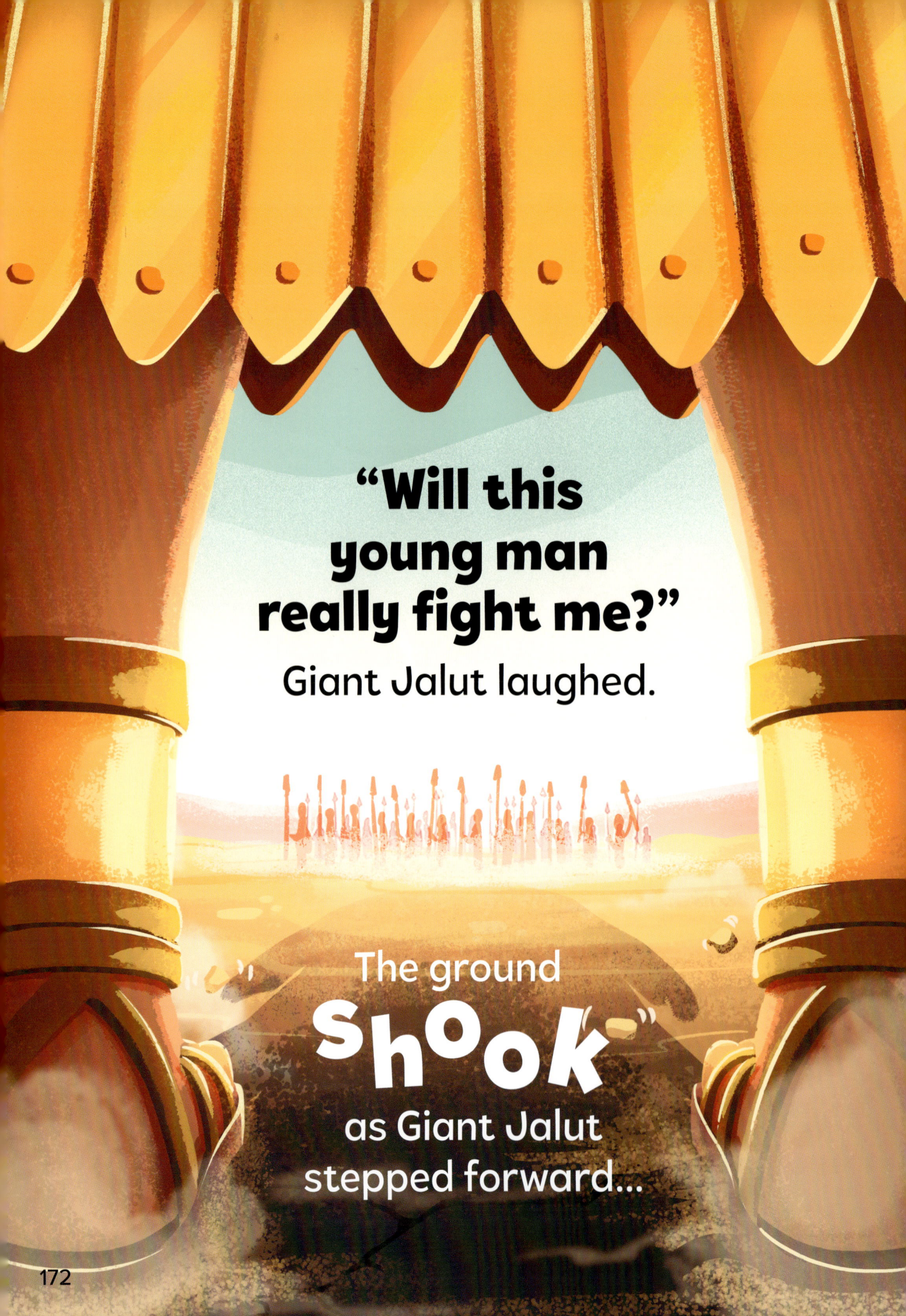

"**Will this young man really fight me?**"

Giant Jalut laughed.

The ground **shook** as Giant Jalut stepped forward...

Dawud put his trust in Allah, with only a slingshot and some stones in his hand.

"BISMILLAH!" said Dawud, as he aimed his shot.

The stone hit Giant Jalut with a mighty thud.

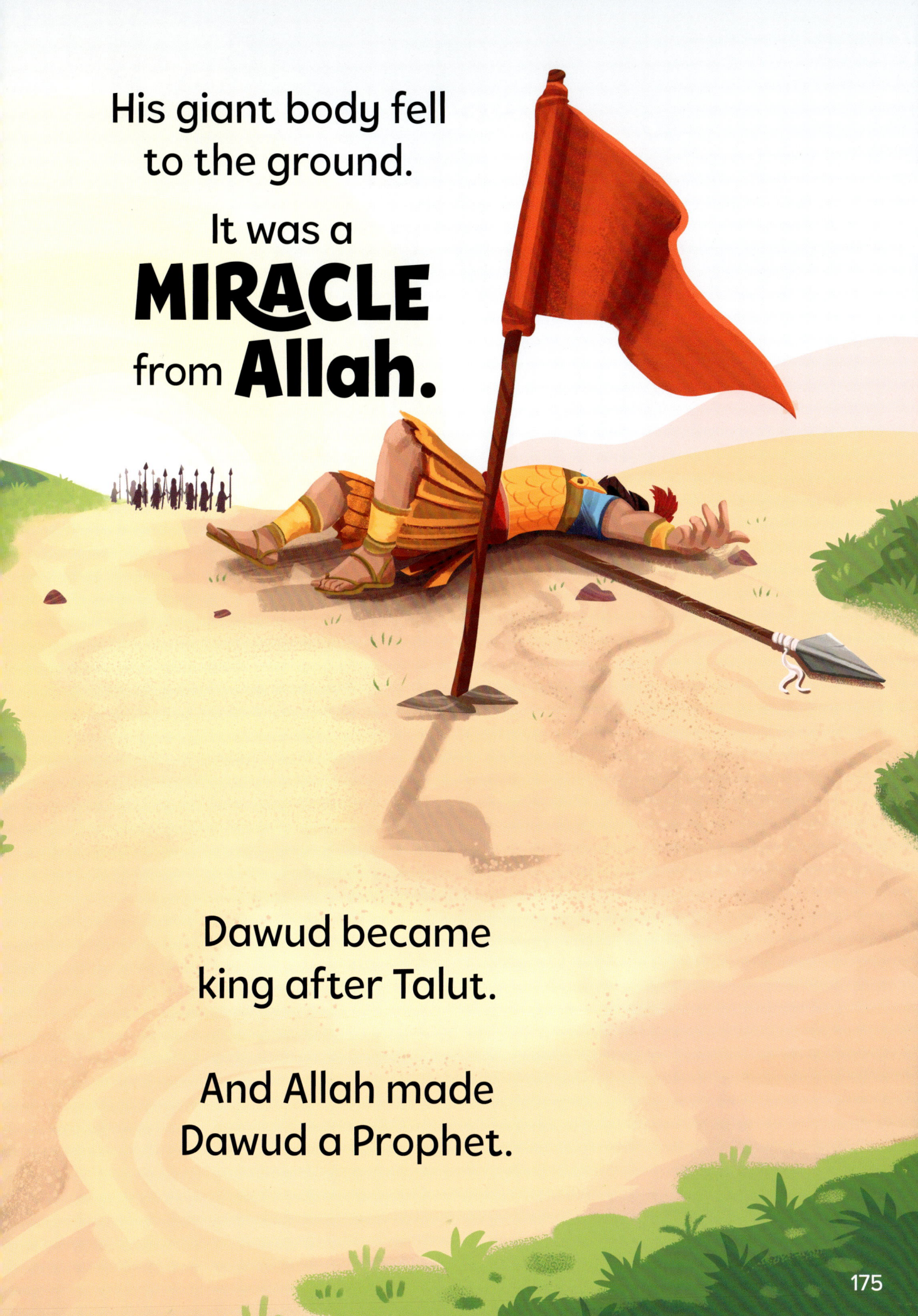

His giant body fell
to the ground.

It was a
MIRACLE
from **Allah.**

Dawud became
king after Talut.

And Allah made
Dawud a Prophet.

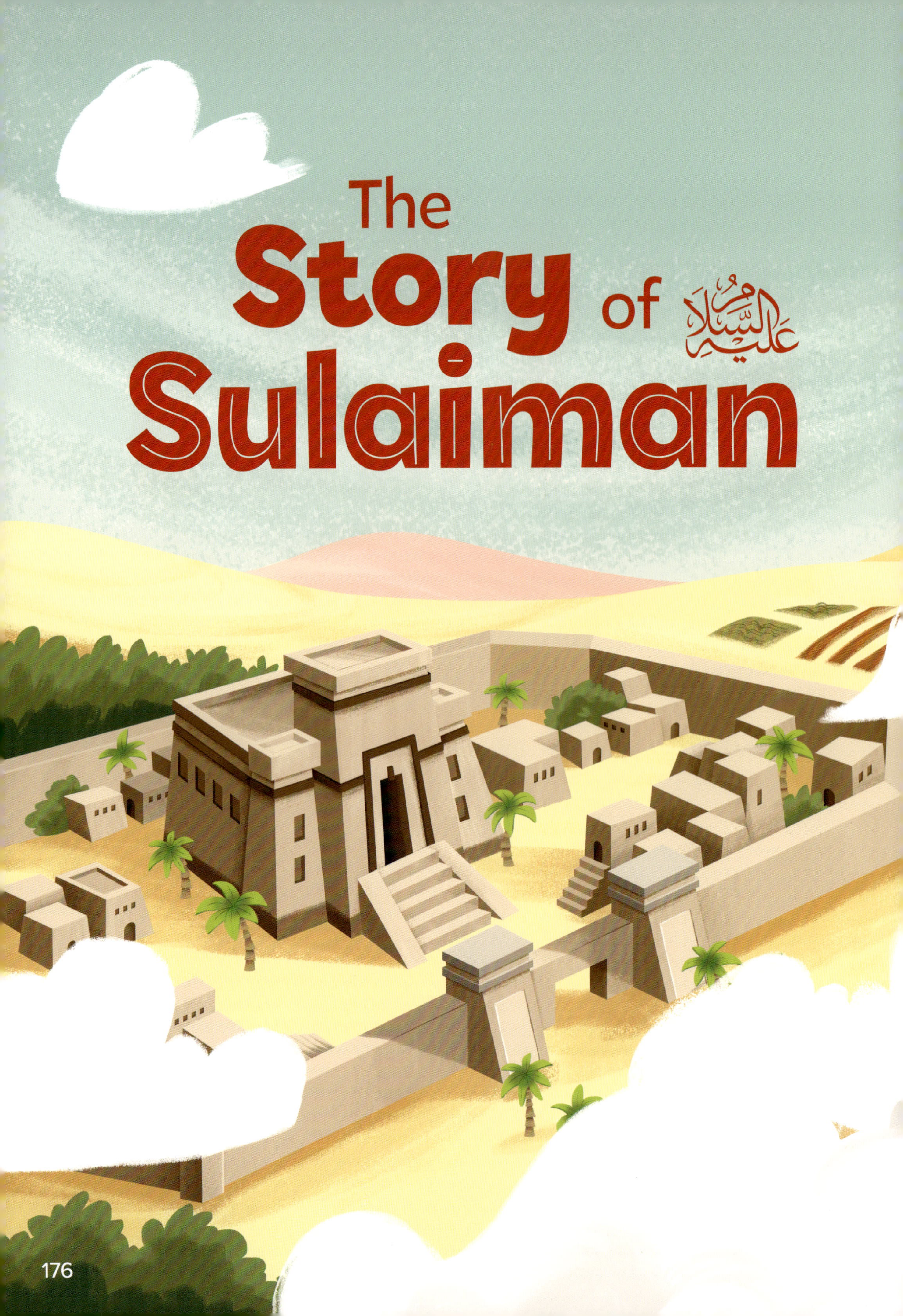

The Story of Sulaiman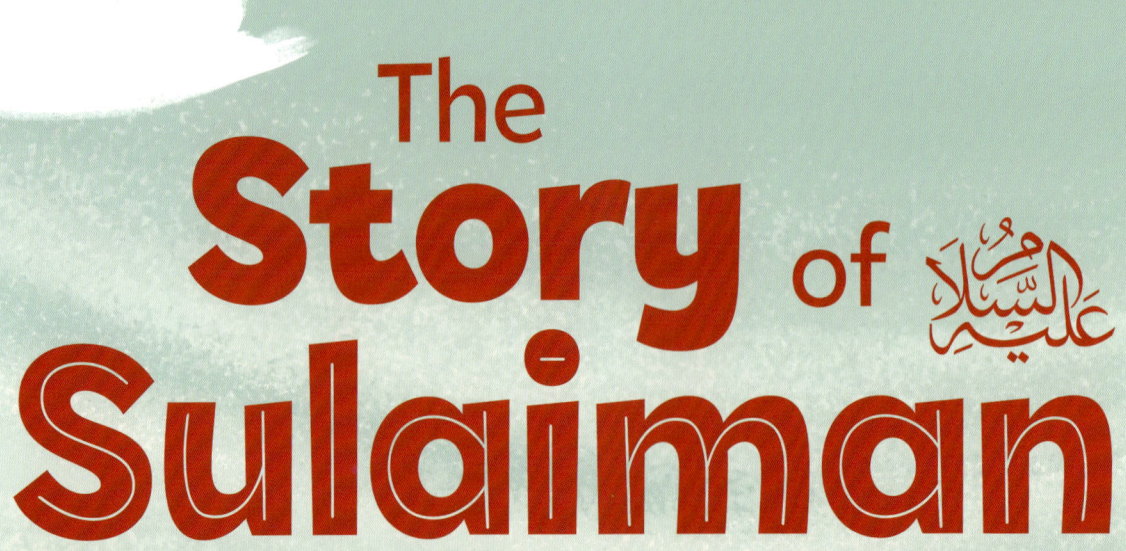

After Prophet Dawud,
his son Sulaiman
ruled Jerusalem.

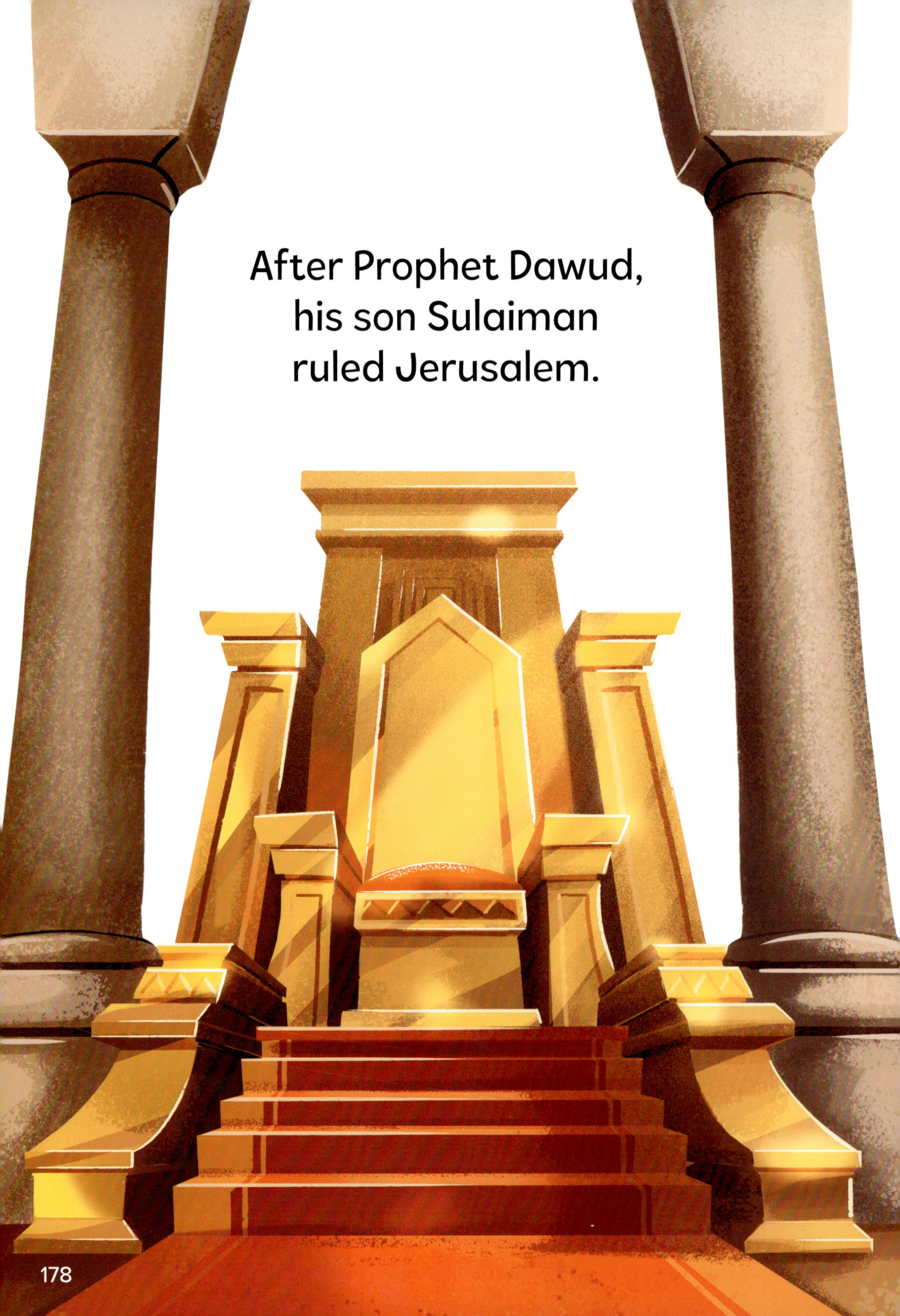

Just like this father,
Sulaiman was also a Prophet
and a wise king.

Allah gave Sulaiman
special powers to
speak to animals
and control the jinns.

One day, Sulaiman's hoopoe bird flew over the mountains and saw a beautiful kingdom called Sheba.

As he flew closer,
the hoopoe saw a queen
and her people praying
to the sun,
instead of Allah.

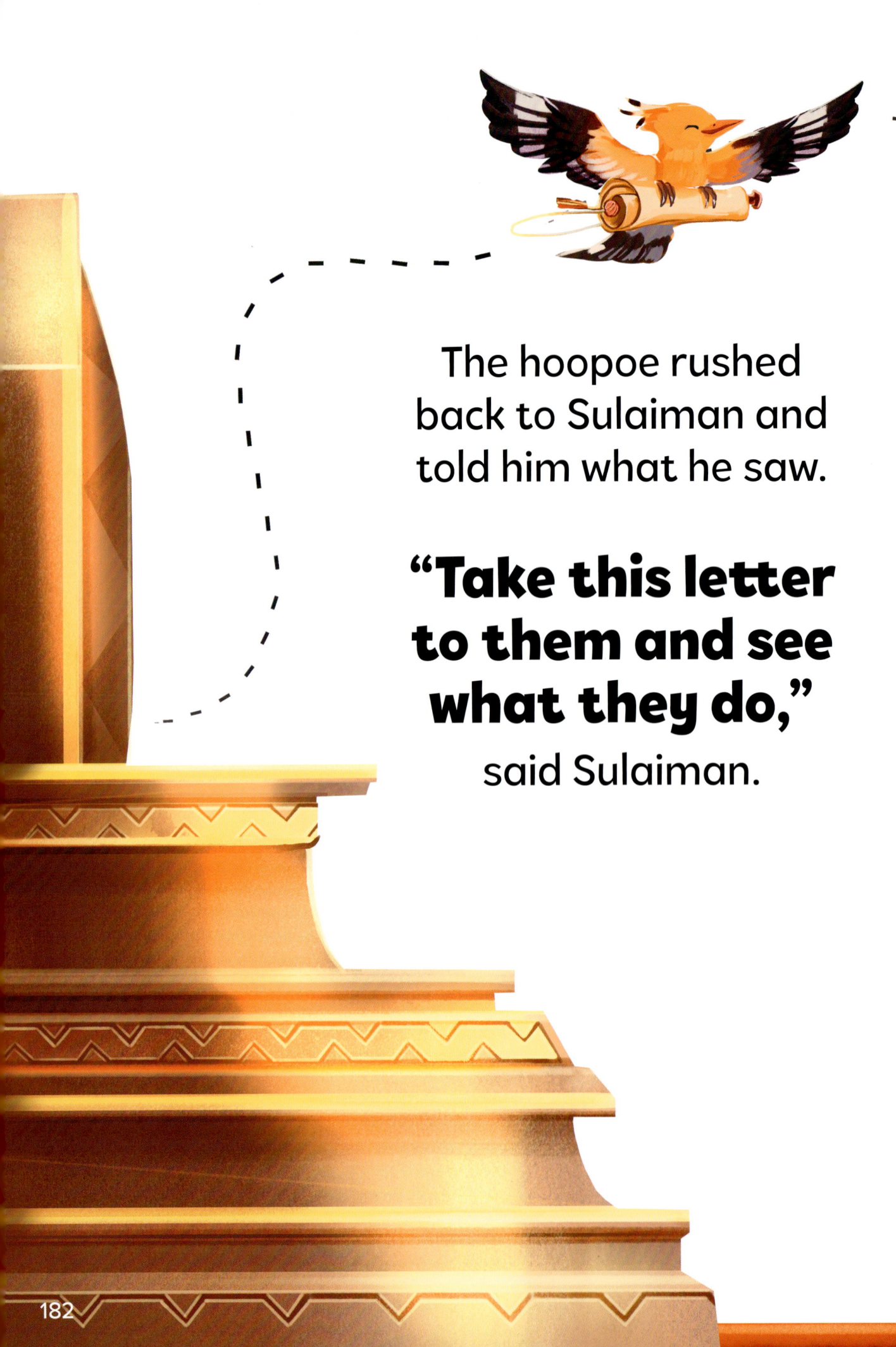

The hoopoe rushed back to Sulaiman and told him what he saw.

"Take this letter to them and see what they do," said Sulaiman.

The hoopoe flew to Sheba and dropped the letter in front of the queen.

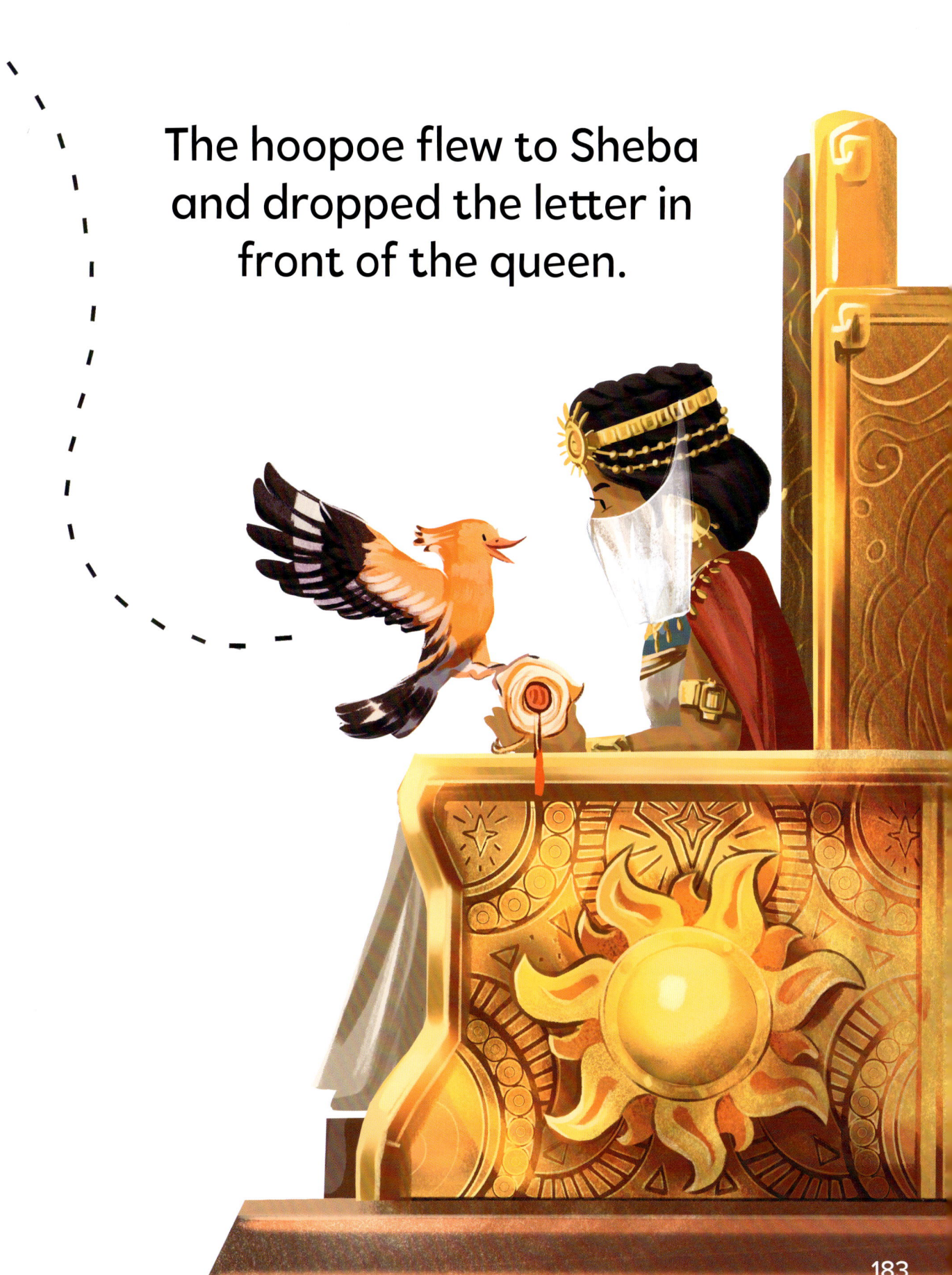

The queen
read the letter.

"In the name of Allah,
the Most Merciful,
the Most Kind.

**Come to me and
submit to Allah.**"

But the queen
did not submit.

Her soldiers were
ready to fight
King Sulaiman.

**But the queen
was wise.**

"I will send Sulaiman
a gift and see what
he does," she said.

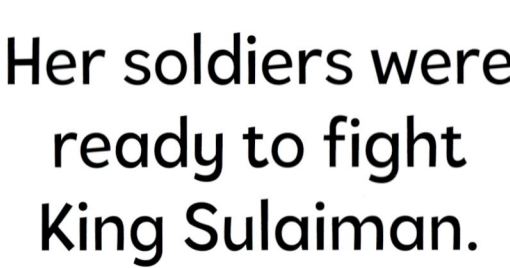

The queen's men brought the gifts to Sulaiman.

"Do you think I need these gifts? What Allah has given me is better," said Sulaiman.

The queen realised that Sulaiman was not trying to take away her kingdom.

But she still did not submit to Allah.

Instead, she set
out to visit
King Sulaiman.

"Who can bring me the queen's throne before she gets here?" Sulaiman asked his soldiers.

"I can bring it in the blink of an eye!" said a jinn.

And just like that, the queen's throne was brought to Sulaiman's palace.

When the queen arrived,
Sulaiman showed
her the throne.

"Does this look like
your throne?" he asked.

"It looks
like mine!"
The queen was amazed.

But she still did not submit to Allah.

Then Sulaiman
asked her to walk on
a floor made of glass.

**The queen
had never
seen anything
like it before.**

"Oh Allah,
I was wrong. I submit
with Sulaiman to You,
the Lord of all creatures,"
said the queen.

And with that, the queen became Muslim and so did her people.

It was a
MIRACLE
from Allah.

The Story of Eesa عليه السلام

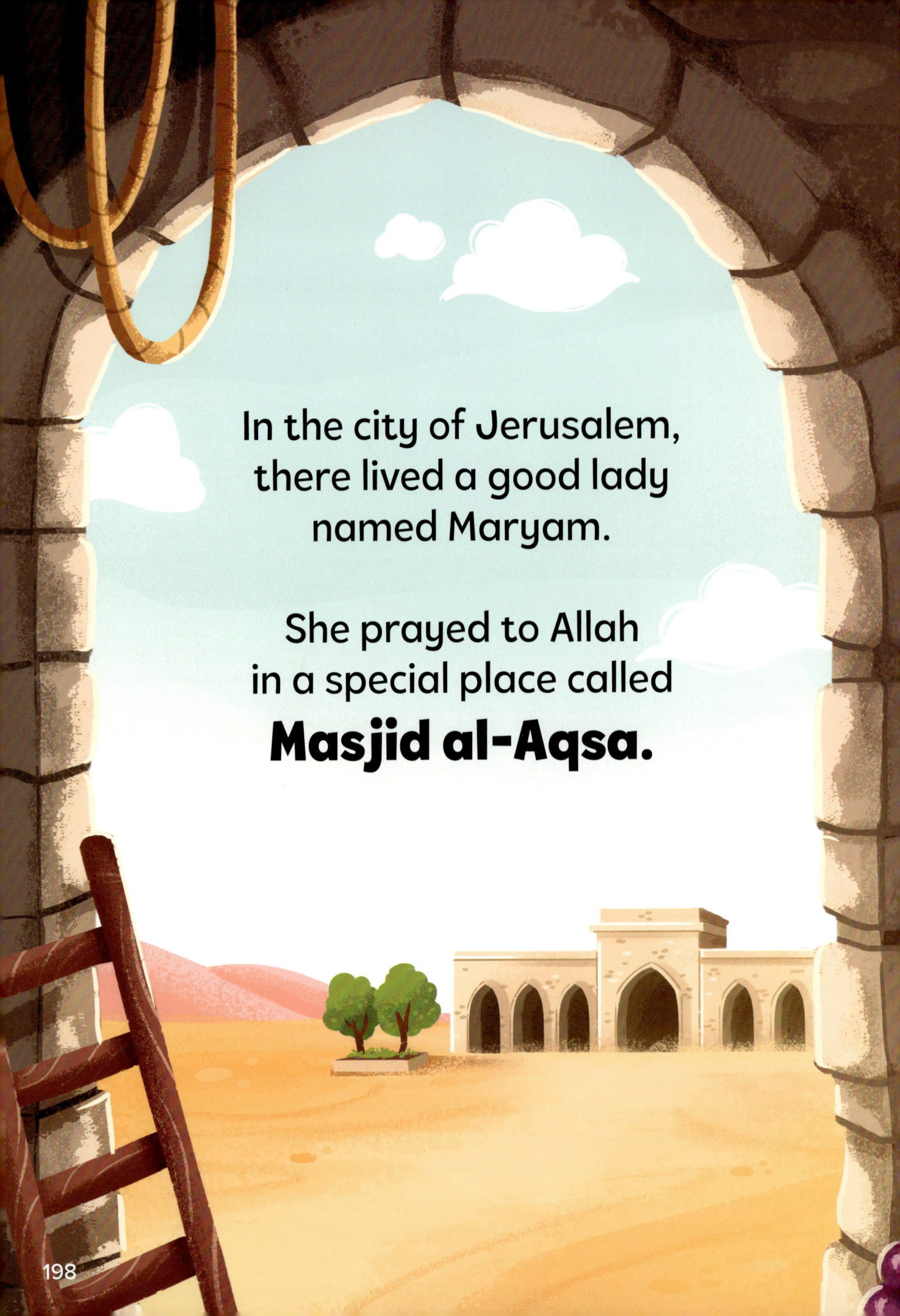

In the city of Jerusalem,
there lived a good lady
named Maryam.

She prayed to Allah
in a special place called
Masjid al-Aqsa.

Allah gave Maryam
special gifts like

lovely
fruits

from lands far away.

He also
sent her a
**special
message.**

Allah sent Angel Jibreel
to give the message
to Maryam.

"Allah gives you **good news** that you will have a baby boy. His name will be Eesa."

Maryam was confused.

She wasn't married. How could she have a baby?

"Allah creates whatever He wants.

He says: 'Be!' and it happens,"

said Angel Jibreel.

Maryam was worried.

What would people think?

But Maryam knew
Allah's plan was best.

Finally, baby Eesa
was born.

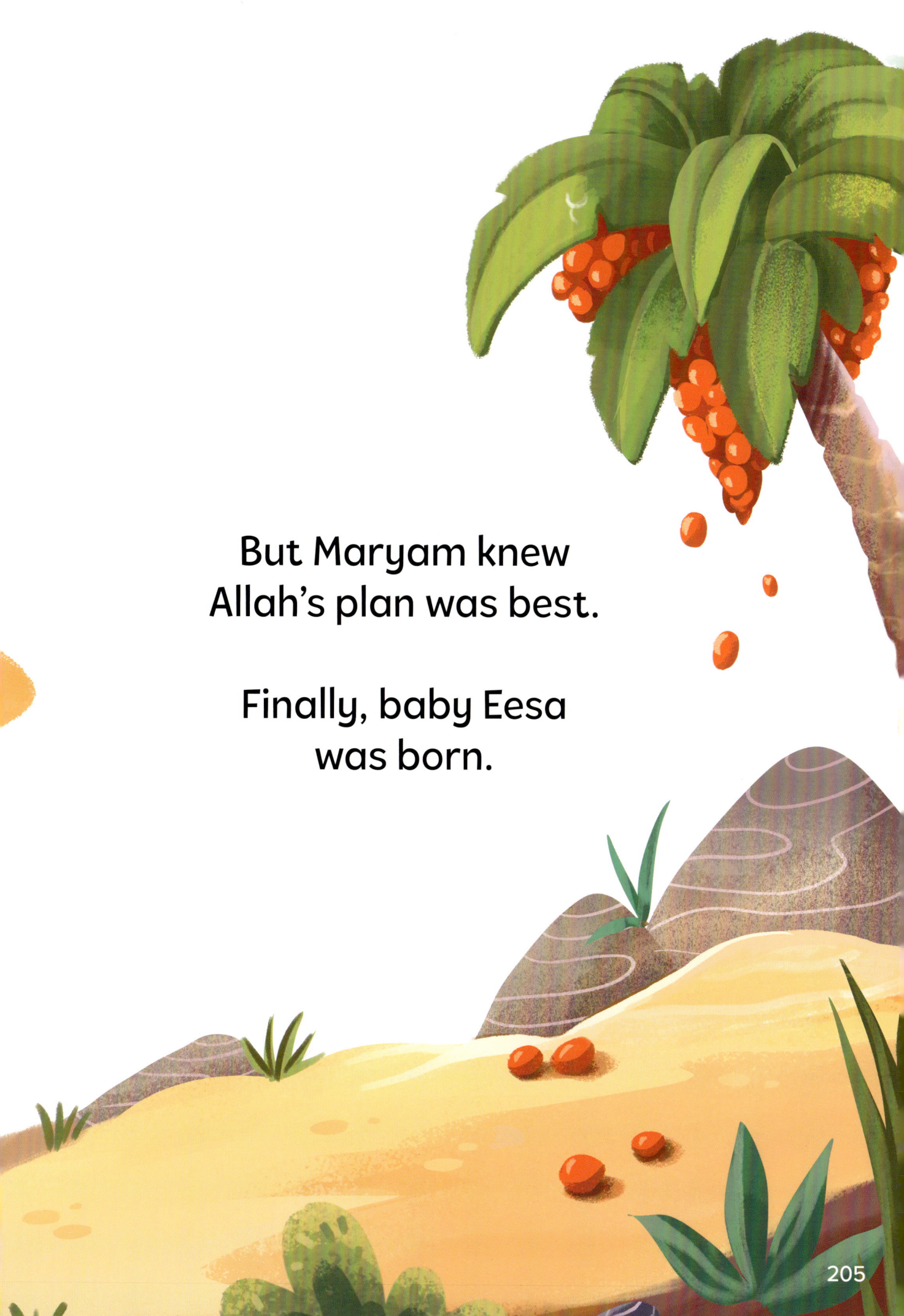

"How come you have a baby?"

the people asked.

Maryam pointed to Eesa without saying a word.

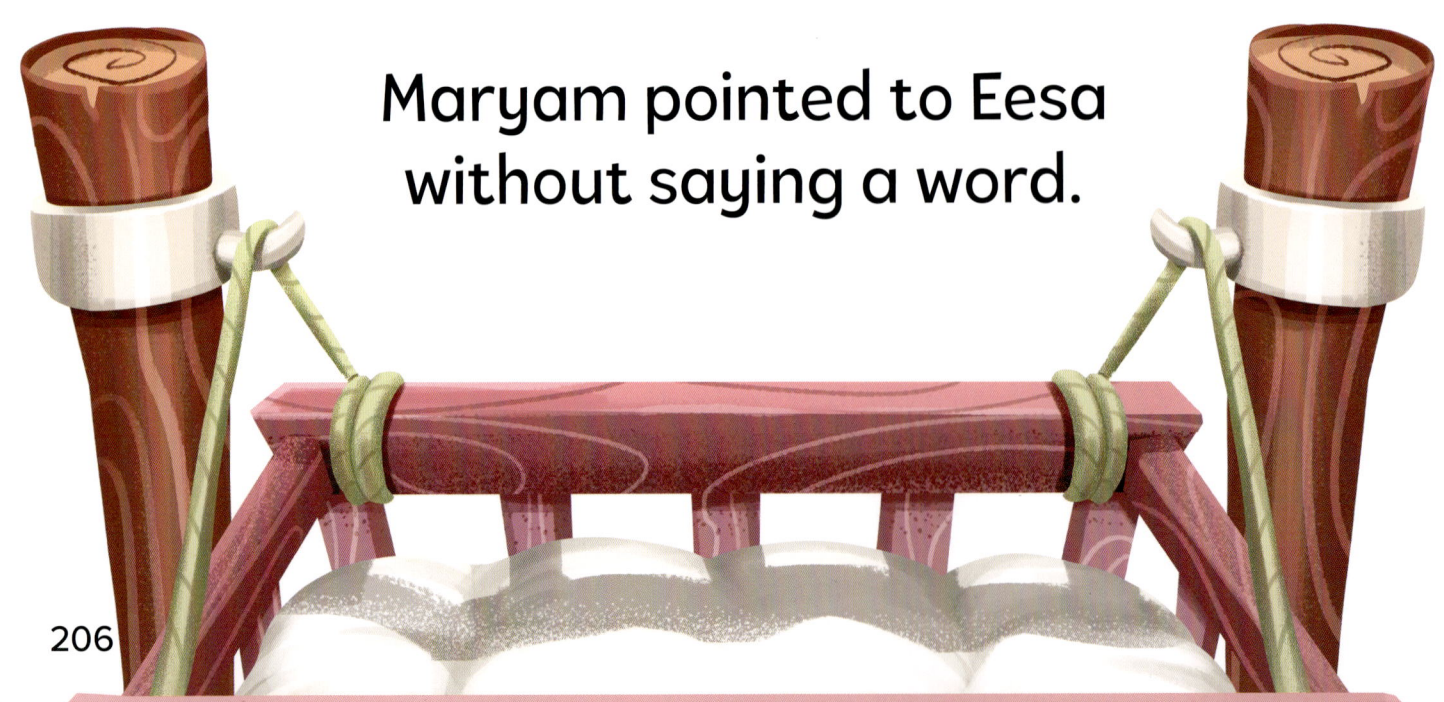

"How can we talk to a baby?"

the people asked.

Baby Eesa spoke,

"I am a servant of Allah ... He made me a Prophet."

As Eesa grew up,
he called his people
to pray to Allah.

But most people
did not listen.

So Allah gave
Eesa miracles.

Prophet Eesa made the **blind** see again.

He made real **birds** from clay.

He brought the dead back to **life.**

It was all by the power of Allah.

The bad people complained
to the king of Jerusalem.

**"Eesa is
tricking people!"**
they said.

So the king's men
came to catch Eesa.

But Allah saved Eesa and raised him up into the Heavens.

It was a
MIRACLE
from **Allah.**

One day, Eesa will come back and help the followers of the final Prophet...

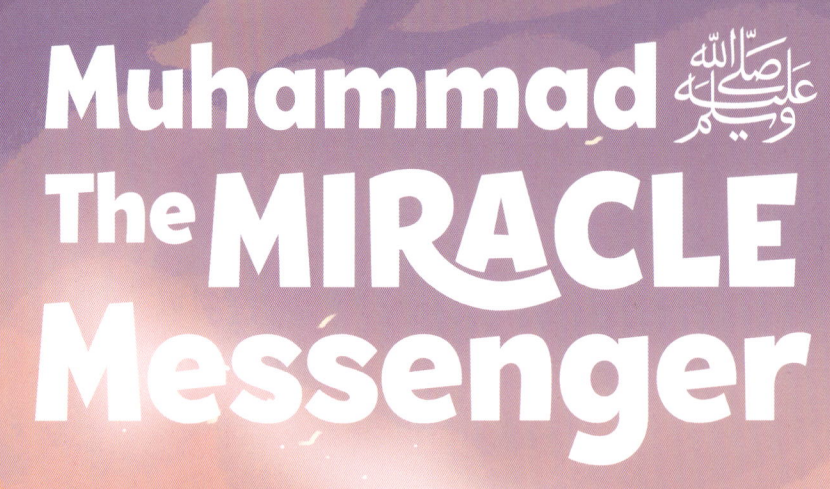

Muhammad ﷺ The MIRACLE Messenger

LEARNING
ROOTS

We pray you enjoyed reading
The Miracles of the Prophets
by Learning Roots.

For more empowering
resources and updates on
the next part of this series,
Muhammad ﷺ
The Miracle Messenger,
please visit:

LearningRoots.com

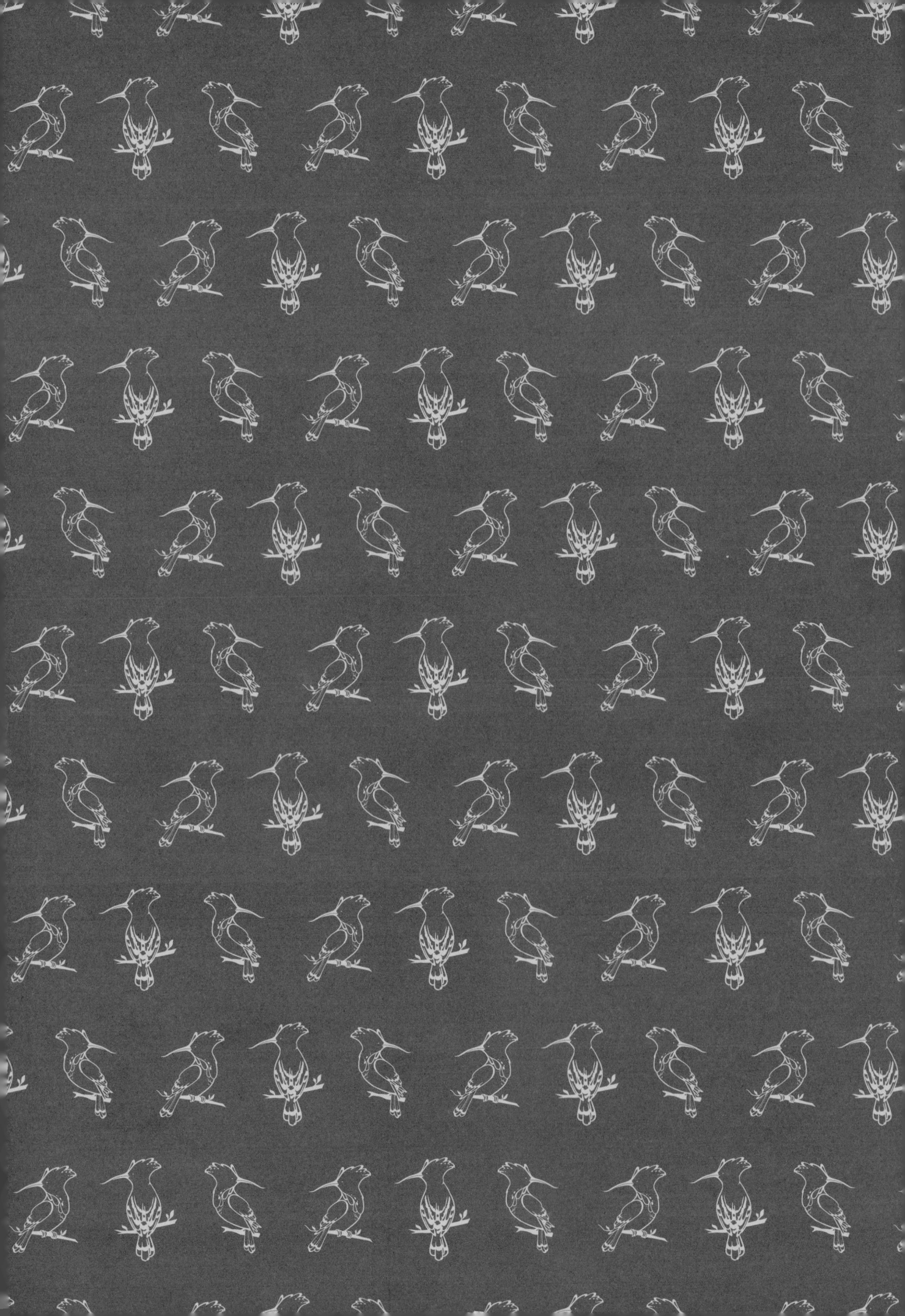